Success Happens!

Let It Happen For You In Network Marketing

DR. TOM BARRETT

Author of the National Best Seller *Dare to Dream and Work to Win*

Success Happens!

Sixth Printing 2009

Published by Business/Life Management, Inc.
ISBN-10:0-9641065-4-X
ISBN-13:978-0-9641065-4-3
Cover design by D Banzon Design

Printed in the United States of America.

Dr. Tom Barrett
Business/Life Management, Inc.
43543 Butler Place
Leesburg, VA 20176

HOW TO ORDER MORE COPIES:

To order more copies, obtain information about quantity discounts, or to order the companion to this book, ***Dare to Dream and Work to Win,*** go to www.daretodream.net

For your convenience order forms are also available in the back of this book.

To Lindsay & Stephanie
(the next generation of entrepreneurs)

You are cleared for take-off

Fly in the direction of your dreams

Love, Dad

CONTENTS

Acknowledgements

The completion of a book is much like success in network marketing...both are team efforts. A team of great people surrounded me while I was writing this book.

Joel Goins – Your knowledge of *how* network marketing works and your respect for the participants in the industry are infectious. You are both my mentor and friend. Thanks for your help with the ideas and manuscripts.

Dr. Bryan Grimmer – Countless times on the golf course you pushed me to keep teaching others what it means to be an entrepreneur and how success is experienced. Thanks for believing in me and in the value of this work.

Joe and Sherry Robinson – Only special people and dear friends take the time to wade through the rough draft of a book. Thank you for your very helpful insights and suggestions. The industry of network marketing is fortunate to have you as an example of how to build a team and a business with vision, hard work, love, and integrity. I am fortunate to call you my friends.

Uma Outka – As the chief editor of *Upline* magazine I was honored to have you be the editor of this book. Your editorial skills and knowledge of network marketing were invaluable assets in this project. Thank you for your constant belief that the contents of this book will be a very significant contribution to our industry. (And thanks for the laughter which made our hard work much more enjoyable.)

Linda Barrett – Thank you for the countless hours you spent listening to my ideas, reading rough drafts, and polishing my work. Like my life, this book would not be complete without you.

My audiences – I have had the honor of training and speaking to many thousands of people in network marketing. My audiences have taught me as much as I have taught them. If you are one of the people that I have spoken to, thank you for your passionate insistence that the ideas and skills in this book are what you need to be successful. Your letters, emails, and verbal affirmations have kept me focused and excited while writing this book. Now that it is finished, may it accelerate the growth of your team and your own personal success.

Introduction

John and I stood looking at the same paintings. He was excited. I was merely intrigued. He looked at the paintings with wonder. I just wondered what he saw that was so captivating. He felt awe. I felt awkward.

I still laugh when I think back to this moment. John was one of the most well-loved and prominent figures in Chicago. He had invited me into his home to get to know me and learn about my career plans. I was 21 years old, just out of college, and clueless about the paintings hanging on his family room wall: three original Norman Rockwells.

Network marketing reminds me of that day John and I looked at the Norman Rockwell paintings together. Some people look at network marketing and readily see its value, wisdom, and potential. Others look at it and wonder why participants in this industry are so excited. Like me, when I was 21 years old, they literally don't understand it. They have no idea what is in front of them.

Why is it so easy not to "see" the strategic genius of network marketing? There are various reasons, some of which have nothing to do with the industry itself. For example:

- Most people have been trained to be employees not entrepreneurs.
- Many people have been given permission to dream but have not been shown how dreams become a reality.
- Many people have been told it is okay to want the most out of life but have not been told how to obtain it.

- Most people know how to work for money, but they have no clue how network marketing can create a revenue stream of money working *for them*.

My assumption is that if you are beginning to read this book you have at least been looking at network marketing and sense there is something to it. My goal in this book is to help you see the genius and potential of this industry.

Another goal of mine, whether you are new to this industry or a veteran, is to give you insights into the mindset of successful people. This book will help you understand how they think, stay focused, and win. It will teach you listening and interactive skills that are indispensable to your success. Additionally, it will teach you things that I have never heard addressed in depth in any network marketing book: the psychology of understanding and managing fear; the hidden dignity of network marketing; and how this industry allows people to create wealth and residual income from two income streams.

For the sake of simplicity, I have chosen to use the term "network marketing" throughout this book even though the term "multi-level marketing" would have been just as appropriate. Similarly, I have selected the term "representatives" to identify participants in network marketing for a very unscientific reason (it can easily be shortened to "rep"). If you or your organization uses the term distributor or consultant, please know that I am using this term to include you as well. "Rep" is simply a less cumbersome word for both the writer and the reader.

Success Happens! is the follow-up to my book, *Dare to Dream and Work to Win*. These books are a two-part series. While you may start with this book if you choose, I suggest you begin with *Dare to Dream and Work to Win* because it provides the foundation that this book builds upon.

Either way, allow me to make one final suggestion before you begin: don't just read these books one time for some brief motivation. To get the most from them read them numerous times. New insights will inevitably come to you with each reading. Join the thousands of team leaders who have used these books as a resource and study guide for their downlines by reading, studying, and discussing each chapter.

My goal in writing is not to inspire you for a moment or two, it is to literally change your thinking and your life. It is to teach you how entrepreneurs think and work; how and why success is possible; and how to enjoy the full measure of success available to you in this extraordinary industry. Anything less would be a goal too small and unworthy of your time or mine. Remember: Success happens. Read on and let it happen for you.

– Tom Barrett, Ph.D.

CHAPTER
ONE

DREAMS: THE ROCKET FUEL OF SUCCESS

The flight attendant leaned forward and quietly whispered to me, "I'm looking for her."

We were on a short one-hour flight from Bemidji, Minnesota to Minneapolis. The commuter jet only carried 31 passengers and I happened to be in the first row. When the flight attendant sat down, she was literally face-to-face and knee-to-knee with me. In a space that small, I thought I might as well have a pleasant time with this person I was looking at directly. After chatting for a few minutes, she shared her search with me.

The flight manifest indicated that one passenger was the same individual who was in the national news that week—a single 21-year-old whose life had instantaneously been irrevocably and dramatically changed. Four days

earlier, she won the entire Powerball Lottery for over 150 million dollars.

When the flight landed, I stood there at baggage claim surveying the small group of passengers trying to guess which individual had just stumbled into wealth. I would have enjoyed meeting this young woman and having the opportunity to congratulate her. I was excited for her because I love to see people win . . . even when it happens only because of luck. Curiously, I could not pick out from this small group of people the one whose life was now so different. Every young woman on the flight looked equally capable of being the winner.

In network marketing, the same thing is true—in a group of ten or 1000 people, everyone is equally capable of being a winner. This is the aspect of our business I find so fascinating. Anyone can have his or her life and financial circumstances wonderfully transformed in this 80 billion dollar per year industry. Age, education, experience, and economics do not determine who sits in the winners' circle. In the pages ahead, you will learn what does.

The lottery attracts people who want instant wealth from massive luck and no effort. By contrast, network marketing attracts people with more realism. They are some of the finest people to be found anywhere. They are often highly motivated, hardworking, open, and honest people who dare to believe that the best of life lies before them. They know it is within their grasp, and they are willing to give their finest efforts to making the success they desire their own personal experience. These people are unseen heroes in the modern-day world. They are not afraid to dream and not afraid to work. All they ask to get started is a level playing field, a fair chance, and the opportunity to get paid what they are worth in the end. Courageously, they want to take their shot at success. And this is precisely what we are all given in a home-based network marketing business.

But I find that most people, including those who come out of the finest MBA programs, have never been taught how successful people work, how entrepreneurs think, and how wealth is earned. Without this knowledge, people often get involved with network marketing, work as hard as they can with total sincerity, and see only minimal results. In the process, success becomes an elusive goal, an unsolved riddle, and a mystery.

So let's take the mystery out of success—right now. Let's make sure that your best efforts are rewarded with the best results. Beginning with this chapter, and for the remainder of this book, you will see how and why you *can* be successful in network marketing.

THE NATURE OF SUCCESS

Success is not nearly as difficult, complicated, or elusive as most people imagine—and it is far more enjoyable than they ever hoped. Indeed, the most extraordinary aspect of success is how insidiously simple it is.

Do you ever wonder what it is that successful people have, or do, that separates them from less successful people? Is it incredible luck or remarkable talent that makes them experience what others wish for but never attain? Happily, success has little to do with excessive luck or talent. Instead, successful individuals share two unique qualities. You need not be innately gifted with these qualities; each of them can be acquired, learned, and developed by anyone.

The two qualities found among successful people are:

1. They have a *dream*.
2. They stay *focused*.

At first glance, these qualities don't seem very impressive. They don't look new, novel, or profound. They have no "sex appeal." Maybe that is why people who want to be successful often overlook them. Let's look at the first quality more closely in this chapter and at the second quality in the next chapter.

SUCCESSFUL INDIVIDUALS HAVE A DREAM

Helen Keller was both deaf and blind. Many years of her life passed before she learned to communicate with others through the help of Ann Sullivan. Long after this breakthrough, Helen Keller was asked, "Is there anything worse than not having sight?" Her response was, "Oh yes, it is to have sight without vision."

I agree with her. Long before most people begin to lose their physical sight, they begin to lose their vision for life. Their ability to dream begins to diminish. Did you ever notice how little children have big dreams and older people have small dreams? Life has the tendency to curtail, rather than cultivate, our ability to dream—and the erosion of this ability is not insignificant. It results in people abandoning hope, accepting the status quo, and achieving far less than they are capable of. In the end, it diminishes the quality and the contribution of their lives.

Why are dreams so important? Because dreams are the blueprint for reality. They are the prototype of things to come. They are the mind's sneak preview of the future. And the more clearly one sees a positive future, the more confidently he or she lives in the present. Realistic dreams have the uncanny ability to engender passion and vigor. They inspire us like rocket fuel, lifting us to new heights and new worlds. This is why Walt Kallestad writes,

"Dreams can help us see the invisible, believe the incredible, and achieve the impossible." Dreams keep the mind clear, the heart hopeful, and the will strong.

In network marketing, dreams are an indispensable part of success. People will often ask me how large the scope of their dreams needs to be. Some believe that their dreams need to be gigantic and full of global vision and impact. They attempt to have a dream that is so large, they wind up being overwhelmed by the scope of it. It paralyzes rather than propels them. Others confuse having a legitimate dream with simply being "a dreamer" (they are not even remotely related). So how big a dream do you need in order to succeed in your business? Does it have to be massive or impressive to others? No. Your dream only needs to be big enough to do four things:

- *You need a dream big enough to get you out of bed in the morning.*
- *You need a dream big enough to keep you up at night.*
- *You need a dream strong enough to get you to ignore fatigue.*
- *You need a dream strong enough to get you to push through fear.*

This is all the dream you need. Anything less is too little; anything more is a bonus.

I thoroughly enjoy being around people with dreams. They have a joy, optimism, and energy about them that is infectious. They inspire me. Hang around these special people long enough and you will discover that dreams fall into four distinct types: *practical* dreams, *fun* dreams, *memorable* dreams, and *significant* dreams.

Practical Dreams

Remember the old expression, "necessity is the mother of invention"? It is a truism. Necessity and practical need are often the catalysts for change. They create movement, stir desire, and force growth. Like a pry bar, they begin to move people who otherwise might not budge out of their circumstances. They get people "off the dime." When people are ready to *do something* about the practical needs in their lives, they can then appreciate that network marketing is the perfect venue for turning practical needs into practical dreams. There are tens of thousands of people who have discovered that in merging their practical needs with network marketing, an entrepreneurial flame sparks in them that they never knew existed. In the process, their lives *and* finances are wonderfully transformed in countless ways.

Practical needs and dreams are like two sides of a coin—and participants in network marketing all have their own reasons for getting started and sticking with this industry. Each reason deserves to be respected and taken seriously. Here are some of the common ones people have shared with me:

COMMON PRACTICAL DREAMS

- I like my job, but I am ready for a new challenge.
- I need to get out of debt.
- I want some supplemental income.
- I want to stop living hand-to-mouth.
- I need to save some money.
- I want to begin getting ready for retirement.

- I need a new car.
- I want a new home.
- I need health insurance.
- I want to be at home more often.
- I want my spouse to not have to work.
- I want the chronic financial pressure to end.

Practical dreams are the most common reason people get involved in network marketing. They provide a perfectly legitimate starting point. In fact, it's my favorite way to see people begin—for several reasons. First, I have great respect for the impact that an extra few hundred dollars per month can have on an individual or family. Additionally, to new participants, the practical dream of earning an extra few hundred dollars per month is both *believable* and *achievable* when they begin, and very *satisfying* after it is achieved. It's then that they usually begin to realize it's *okay* to expand their beliefs, dreams, and expectations in network marketing.

Enjoy your practical dreams. Make sure you have some that are clear, tangible, important to you, and attainable. Let them be the fuel source that keeps you moving away from where you are and toward the place you want to be.

Fun Dreams

Fun dreams are just like they sound—fun! As people begin to move beyond just barely surviving financially, they begin to give themselves permission to have some fun dreams. And fun dreams are very important. They energize and uplift us. They give us something to look forward to and work toward. Just thinking about the fun things we intend to do or have can change our disposition. They serve a significant positive purpose.

Usually, fun dreams require disposable income, and many people's financial margins are so tight that there is no room for the fun or frivolous things in life. (Or they do what is fun when they cannot really afford to do so. This only increases their financial debt and pressure and creates stress, not satisfaction.) Millions of people are so financially constrained that they have no serious expectation of realizing fun dreams *ever*. Month after month, they struggle to simply keep up with their seemingly ever-increasing expenses: car, rent or mortgage, utilities, clothing, school, etc. While doing this, they hope to set some money aside so that they can take a modest vacation or two during the year. Do this long enough, and it is easy to see why people abandon their fun dreams. They know they are caught in a cycle of beginning each year with the hope of getting ahead and ending each year just struggling to keep up. Let's explore why this happens.

Money is really a very simple commodity. There are only five things we can do with it:

THE FIVE WAYS THAT MONEY IS UTILIZED

1. Money can be used to pay debt.
2. Money can be used to pay taxes.
3. Money can be spent.
4. Money can be given away.
5. Money can be saved or invested.

Do you ever find yourself asking, "Where did all my money go?" Without exception, it went into one of these five categories. What happens to the income of most hardworking individuals? Look at the list above. The first two, paying debt and taxes, are nonnegotiable. They have to be paid. When combined, they take a significant percentage of most people's income. The remaining percentage is quickly consumed in category three. It is spent on "the stuff of life," the routine monthly expenses. For many people, the first three categories leave little room for the last two categories of giving and saving. This constant rapid dispersion of limited money results in people moving fun dreams so far down on their priority lists that they finally fall off. There simply is not enough cash flow to allow for this important category. This is why many people begin with practical dreams when they start in this business. This is all they can see!

Many people have spent so many years "just getting by" financially that truly envisioning fun dreams is far outside their worldview. Initially, they cannot comprehend having or doing things simply for fun. It is a skill they need to redevelop. Others feel "false guilt" because a fun personal dream seems too indulgent or not meaningful enough. Trust me—if you apply what is in this book, you will have sufficient revenue for all four types of dreams and be able to use your money in all five ways.

Personally, I always have a clear list of all four types of dreams. I love checking off the dreams I've completed and replacing them with new ones. What is my next fun dream? Without doubt it is completely frivolous. It developed while I was speaking for a network marketing group in Milwaukee, Wisconsin. While I was there, I was reminded that this city is the corporate headquarters for one of the most famous motorcycle manufacturers in the world: Harley-Davidson. I also learned that the city hosts an annual parade of Harley owners that is unbelievably fun to be a part of. Additionally, I was informed that in the near future, the 100-year anniversary of Harley-Davidson is taking place and that there will be over one hundred thousand Harley-Davidson riders in this parade. Everyone expects it to be the "granddaddy of all parades." Guess who will be one of them? That's right, I am buying a Harley because I plan to be in the parade. Is this dream of major significance? No. Is it practical? No. Is it meaningful? Not really. So why will I do it? Because I can and because it will be great fun. That's reason enough!

> ***"A dream is the first indispensable requirement of success."***

I often kid my friends that I work hard so that I can play hard. And I certainly do my share of both of these. Let's face it—if you have time and no money, or money and no time, then you are not really free to fully enjoy life. We need both of these simultaneously. This is why I am such a strong proponent of network marketing—this industry that gives anyone a shot at achieving practical dreams and having the time and revenue to enjoy the fun ones.

So learn to dream again! Allow yourself to begin to have some fun dreams. Write them down, talk about them, and let them give you joy even prior to their achievement. It is amazing how they begin to enrich the color and improve the flavor of daily life. Don't be embarrassed or feel guilty for having fun dreams. It doesn't matter how silly or frivolous they may seem to others. They are your dreams and you need to give yourself the authority to enjoy your success in your own style.

As we will see later, one of the hidden dignities of this industry is the freedom it gives people—freedom beyond time and money. It frees people from pressure, anxiety, worry, and constraint. When these are eliminated, what often emerges is a personality that has long been squelched by the vice-grip of economic stress. What is rediscovered is a person's ability to laugh, love, flex, forgive, serve, and roll with the punches in life. Network marketing frees people to be their very best selves—and that's not a small freedom.

Memorable Dreams

Do you have a wish list? Are there some truly special things you would like to do or places you would like to go in your lifetime? These are what I call memorable dreams.

Memorable dreams are similar to fun dreams but far more meaningful. They are the landmark moments or experiences of life that stand out above many others. We anticipate our memorable dreams with great expectation and remember them fondly forever. We never forget them because they are in a league of their own. They stand head and shoulders above many other rich moments in life.

In network marketing, it is very common and appropriate for people to begin to dream again, even at the level of memorable dreams. This is a natural byproduct of understanding the extraordinary efficiency, power, and profitability of network marketing. The size and scope of their dreams increase in direct proportion to their expectation of success.

Although I am a strong advocate of remembering the simple pleasures of life, I also know that it often requires money to create memories—it's a good thing that the financial rewards of success in network marketing are so significant as to make memorable dreams possible!

Friends with grown children often joke that it takes money to get quality time with their children. For example, many parents eagerly await their kids' return home from college. Although they've been anticipating the chance to see and be with the children they love, it quickly dawns on these parents that grown children are swiftly satiated in the amount of time they need with mom or dad. They want to say hello, drop off their laundry, get a quick bite to eat, and then go visit their friends—the people who are "really fun" to be with. Against this backdrop, it is a tough sell to say, "Hey, why don't you hang around here this evening. We will grill some burgers and watch a video or play some games." An invitation like this rarely inspires a response of, "It doesn't get any better than that. Count me in! I'll call my friends right now and cancel my plans."

The same is true of married children. They are understandably busy with their own lives. When parents call them and suggest that they drop by for the evening or come visit for a weekend, it is easy for their children to feel too busy, tired, etc. to take them up on the offer.

There are things, however, that *will* get the attention of busy kids. Call them and tell them you are going skiing for a week, or on a cruise or safari, or overseas, and that you would like them to join you at no cost to them. You will be amazed at how these terribly busy people suddenly can clear their schedules for an entire week! It takes money to make some memories. Networkers understand that success in this business allows them this: the ability to live life to the fullest, to laugh, have fun, and enjoy making memories with people they love. Believe me, it makes all the hard work in network marketing abundantly worthwhile in the end. And it is the power of our dreams that drives us forward while we work and wait for our expectations to become reality.

Significant Dreams

The fourth type of dream is the most satisfying and meaningful of all to me. I call these *significant* dreams. These dreams can cost the least amount of money but have the greatest impact on the lives of those we meet and care about. Do you remember the old AT&T ads that ended with, "Reach out and touch someone"? This is the essential motivation behind significant dreams. They are simply about looking for ways to touch the lives of others. I've found that few things are more satisfying than this, whether our impact is large or small.

One of the primary reasons I enjoy being affiliated with the industry of network marketing is because of the quality of people it attracts. I have never met another group of people with a greater penchant for significant dreams—and my professional life keeps me in regular contact with the upper echelons of the political, corporate, and Internet worlds. Ask people in this industry *why* they stay so focused and work so diligently and you will be impressed with the nobility, kindness, and care that drive them. Here are a few examples:

- The pastor of a small church whose dream is to make enough money in his home-based business to be able to serve his congregation for free. He will then take the money they pay him and hire an assistant pastor. This way, they will be able to help a greater number of people.
- The physician who is growing her business so she can continue to render free medical service to those in need.

- The countless people who work a full-time job during the day and a home-based business at night to improve the quality of life for their families.
- The couple who grew a very successful network marketing business to build a hospice that gives free care to the terminally ill.
- The dentist that developed her network marketing business so she and her husband could travel for months at a time to give free dental care to people in underdeveloped countries.

Bernie Lavery epitomized for me all that is good about this industry—he represented the new era of professionals embracing network marketing. Bernie got started in network marketing when he was in his fifties and already retired. He had a Ph.D. from Penn State in biochemistry and worked in senior management with Dupont for 30 years. He was successful and financially set for life. He had no monetary need to get in this business. Why did he? Because he understood the power of residual income and he absolutely loved helping others see the wisdom of network marketing. I golfed with him one Friday last year, had dinner with him and his wife that evening, spent the night in his home, and did a training for his network marketing organization the next day. We played, laughed, and dreamed together. He was in love with his family and with life. He never once boasted about his prior professional and financial success. Do you know what he was most proud of and talked about the most? The fact that his daughter had joined him in his network marketing business so she could stay home with her newborn baby. He was so excited for her and his grandchild! Regrettably, Bernie passed away the Wednesday after I was with him. His love for his family, this industry, and the joy of helping others will never be forgotten by those of us fortunate enough to call him our friend. He knew what it was to have a significant dream.

THE RED HERRING IN NETWORK MARKETING

I was a total cynic when I first began to research this industry. I was sure only a complete fool would get involved with it. I was certain it was barely legal, barely credible, barely profitable, and barely worth anyone's time. However, after thorough analysis, I realized I could not have been more wrong. I was astonished to see what an ingenious business model network marketing is and how it allows customers, corporations, and participants all to benefit. It is the ultimate win-win-win.

But there is one huge problem in network marketing—a red herring. It is a deficiency that is too serious to be ignored, and it doesn't matter how good your particular company is, this problem exists in yours too. It has to be squarely faced. Both futures and fortunes hang in the balance until this lethal problem is resolved.

But before we face this problem, let me ask you some questions that will initially seem "off the wall":

- The night before Christmas, what is a parent's worst nightmare when frantically wrapping gifts at 2:00 a.m.? What words can they see on the outside of a box that will strike fear in their hearts? You guessed it: *Batteries Not Included.*
- Did you ever buy a new car, or a new "used car," from a dealership and notice that they gave it to you with the gas gauge on empty? Don't you wonder why you can pay thousands of dollars for your vehicle and they won't even pop for a full tank of gas? How cheap can you get!

- Did you ever get invited to a party and at the bottom of the invitation it said, "B.Y.O.B."?

Each of these seemingly irrelevant and unrelated questions illustrates the red herring in network marketing. They depict the problem we must face and the void we must fill. In network marketing, the batteries are not included; the fuel tank is empty; it's B.Y.O.B. It is singularly your responsibility to keep the batteries charged and the fuel tank full. Also, network marketing is B.Y.O.D., B.Y.O.P., and B.Y.O.R. You're invited to the party, but:

Bring Your Own Dream

Bring Your Own Passion

Bring Your Own Reason

Nobody can supply these for you. This is why having a dream that is clear and personal is so imperative. Dreams keep us charged up. They keep us well fueled for a long life-changing journey. They give us our passion, our reason, and our relentless drive to keep going. In short, dreams give us direction and determination; focus and fuel; perseverance and perspective. Maybe this is why Steve Schulz, one of the premiere examples of success in our industry, reminds us that, "dreams make you bulletproof."

This is also why a dream is the first indispensable requirement of success in *any* significant endeavor. It is the rocket fuel that propels every entrepreneur forward. The more clear, palpable, and personal your dream is, the more it will sustain you in the inevitable moments when fatigue suggests you rest, fear suggests you run, and people you know suggest you are crazy.

Allow yourself to dust off the skill of dreaming. Remember what Tom Mathews, who makes millions of dollars each year in network marketing, often says: “It is impossible to exceed your wildest dreams unless you have some wild dreams!” Let yourself have some dreams that are practical, fun, memorable, and significant. Not only will they transform your life in the future, they will enrich it in the present by infusing it with legitimate hope, joy, purpose, and direction.

When you take your dream (Success Quality #1) and combine it with staying focused (Success Quality #2), you will begin to understand why success is so insidiously simple and well within your reach. We’ll explore focus in the next chapter.

CHAPTER
TWO

FOCUS: HOW FORTUNES ARE MADE

Without doubt, two of the most colorful, gifted, and fascinating people I have ever met are Mike and Monza Cornell. (How many people do you know who would move to a remote mountain area, build a tee-pee and live in it for two years, learn from the local Indians how to live off the land, and then do so for eight years with no running water, plumbing, or electricity!) Just prior to beginning their network marketing career, Mike and Monza owned and operated one of the most successful fitness gyms on the West Coast. Their client roster was a "who's who" of Hollywood. They were the fitness experts and trainers to movie stars, media people, and others for whom looking their best is an integral part of their success.

Every year, like clockwork, Mike and Monza witnessed the same amusing pattern. In January, they would be

flooded with new clients applying for membership in their fitness center. Routinely, these new clients would sign up for the club and pay their membership fees. They would tell Mike or Monza, "*This* is the year, *this* is the time that I am going to get into shape." They were going to look good, feel good, and be good. They were excited, eager, and open to the idea of getting into fighting form. Just the thought of their physical transformation got them pumped up. They were going to stop feeling awful and begin to look awesome. They had a dream. They had a desire. They had a goal. They could hardly wait to get started. Or . . . could they?

With comic predictability, over 90 percent of these same people would stop showing up for their workouts within 30 days of joining the club! What happened? Of their own volition, they had shown up, signed up, and paid up; they were not coerced into anything; it was *their* desire and ambition to look and feel their best; this is what they wanted for themselves. So how could they sign up with such a positive attitude and then promptly abandon their own goals? How could they have world-class trainers available to them and not take advantage of their expertise? How could they begin pursuing what they wanted for themselves and then quit before they had the satisfaction of seeing results?

It's this same pattern in action when people:

- buy fitness equipment for their home but never use it
- buy jogging shoes but never run
- buy books but never read them
- buy tapes but never listen to them
- intend to learn a musical instrument but never practice
- intend to learn a language but never attend a class

- intend to learn to use a computer or the Internet but never do
- intend to make time for a hobby but never do
- intend to learn new professional skills but never take continuing education
- think of staying in touch with people they care about but never get around to it
- think of taking action on a good business idea but never quite get started
- think of writing a book but never sit down to write
- desire to lose weight but never diet or exercise
- desire to effectively manage their money but never change their spending habits
- desire to get their home, office, or life organized but never conquer the chaos

It also happens in network marketing. It is not uncommon for people to "show up, sign up, pay up" and then do almost nothing with the business they were so eager to join. They exit the opportunity that could have been their entrée into an entirely different life.

Have you ever seen someone join your team who had phenomenal potential, exceptional talent, and clearly expressed dreams or desires? You went home and thought, "Oh, have I got a player now! This guy will be huge in the business! I have finally found that one person that everyone in our industry dreams of finding. I love this business." Ten days later, that same individual stops coming to meetings, is slower to return your calls, and begins to be "too busy" to grow his business. What happened? He balked when his dream required discipline, his expectations required effort, and his desired future required daily focus.

No matter how big, exciting, or life changing someone's dream is, without the ability to focus, that dream will never materialize. A dream *wished* for is very different from a dream *worked* for. The dilemma for many people who honestly long to be successful entrepreneurs and business owners is that they have no experience exercising daily focus.

WHY PEOPLE DON'T FOCUS... FOR LONG

Do you ever wonder why people have so much trouble staying focused? There are numerous reasons why, and we will explore them more throughout this book. But there is one primary reason for this common phenomenon. Most people have never been taught the importance and skill of staying focused.

For example, loving parents in countless families repeatedly tell their children how talented and capable they are and that they can be almost anything they want to be in life. Of course, these are important refrains for a young child to grow up hearing, but what these well-meaning parents frequently overlook is the importance of also teaching them that talent and ability only produce success when combined with focus. As a result, many young people enter the adult work world with a general sense of ability, but no particular sense of how to translate that into direction, productivity, and success.

Similarly, the corporate world and most business schools emphasize business models, management theory, market trends, brand identity, and revenue streams, while providing little or no guidance in how to see projects through to completion. This is no small oversight—the ability to sustain focus is where fortunes are won and lost every day both in the corporate world and in network marketing. Focus is what separates winners from wishers, and in network marketing, the ability to remain focused is the single most important element of success. In our industry, I will gladly trade you ten people with grand dreams and prodigious talent for one individual with a small dream, modest talent, and a relentless ability to stay focused. In the end, that one will run circles around all of his or her more highly gifted and big-dreaming colleagues.

NETWORK MARKETING IS LIKE GETTING A DOCTORATE

In doctoral education, one quickly becomes familiar with the term "A.B.D."—it stands for "all but dissertation," and designates individuals who were admitted into a Ph.D. program and successfully completed all of the class work, but never completed the doctoral dissertation. There are thousands of people with this designation. With the ambition to apply and the intellectual ability to be admitted to a doctoral program, how can they not finish? Why do they spend thousands of dollars and years of their lives taking classes and then quit before receiving their degree?

It is because completing class work is vastly different from completing a dissertation. At the doctoral level, class work is the easy part. It is simply a more rigorous version of a routine they've already been doing for years. All that is necessary is to plug into the rhythm and structure of higher education: attend classes, take notes, read extensively, write papers, and take exams. Repeat this process with each required class and you can complete the structured part of a doctoral curriculum.

But when it comes to writing a doctoral dissertation, there is no structure to plug into. There is no routine and rhythm, no classes to attend, no tracks to run on. There is no one to give you a schedule, tell you what to do, when to do it, or how to do it. There is no one to hold your hand. You are on your own and expected to be capable of being a self-starter. It is this lack of mandated structure that causes so many to flounder rather than flourish. It exposes an inability to sustain internal focus without external structure. This inability results in some of the world's most gifted people falling far short of their own aspirations.

Like doctoral candidates, the Achilles heel of many people in network marketing is the inability to sustain personal focus. They do not know how to master the art of staying on task unless someone else is their taskmaster. Many in our industry could be designated "A.B.D." It would not stand for "all but dissertation"—it would stand for "all but discipline." The result would be the same: Dreams unrealized and talent never utilized.

Ironically, personal freedom is the most appealing aspect of network marketing for many people. They desire the freedom to work their own hours, be their own boss, make their own decisions, and pursue their own aspirations. They are weary of being told what to do and when to do it. They want to take charge of their own lives! What a surprise when they discover that they cannot manage the very freedom they so adamantly desired.

FOCUS IS NOT A TALENT

One of my dearest friends is also a shrink. It is not uncommon for us to dream, plan, and work together. He is often the first to know about many of my business and professional activities. When he hears about various things I am involved in, he will often look at me and say, "Barrett, you are the most focused individual I have ever met." My response to him is always the same: "Walt, you treat my ability to stay focused as if it were a gift or a talent. It is not. It is a decision."

Focus is not an innate capacity that you either have or do not have—it is not something you are born with. Consequently, it is something you can acquire. Focus is a skill and a habit you can develop. Like success, there is nothing mysterious or complicated about it. Boring as it may be, focus is the simple act of staying on task. It is simply doing what you need or intended to do.

"The ability to stay focused is not a gift or a talent. It is a decision."

There is an ancient proverb that says, "In all toil there is profit. But mere talk tends only to want." That is a gentle way of saying that talk is cheap. Profit and wealth come to those who quietly and diligently do what is before them each day. They stay focused. They are constantly aware of what they want in the future and do what is necessary, on a daily basis, to move them incrementally closer toward their goals.

A common misconception is that successful people don't wrestle with the same things that less successful people wrestle with each day. The assumption is that successful people are always eager and motivated to do what is necessary to get ahead. In reality, successful people wrestle with all of the same things that less successful people wrestle with—*they just win more of the battles.*

Let's look at some routine networking tasks and see how successful people handle them. In our industry, there are phone and e-mail messages to check and respond to, prospects to contact or follow up with, people on your team who need help growing their businesses, questions to answer, problems to solve, meetings to plan, arrange, attend, and lead. These are the common activities of anyone intent on growing a successful network marketing business. (Coincidentally, they are also common activities for senior executives in the corporate world.) The moment of decision—to do or not to do—occurs when these common tasks arise and there is no desire to do them. For example:

- What do successful people do at the end of an already long day when they are tired and ready to stop working, but realize they still have to check their messages and make several calls?
- What do successful people do in the evening when they intended to contact three prospects about their business but feel weary . . . and realize there is a good movie on television?
- What do successful people do when they have had a stressful day in their regular job and now it is time to attend a network marketing meeting or sit in on a conference call?
- What do successful people do when their plate is already full with their own life struggles and someone in their downline wants to talk with them about problems they are having in their business?
- What do successful people do when they are tired from talking to people all day long and someone in their downline calls wanting them to do a three-way call with a prospect?

In each of these situations, successful people experience normal battles within themselves. They have the same thoughts and feelings any of us would: "I'm tired. I don't want to make that call. I don't want to talk to that person. I don't want to hear about another problem. I don't want to go to another meeting. I don't want to talk to one more misinformed skeptic who will ask, 'Is this is a pyramid scheme?' What I really want to do is rest and relax. I want to kick back and get lost in a movie or a good book. I want to ignore these last few things that I know should be done today."

If successful people have all the same battles that less successful people have, what makes them so different? What makes them different is *their response* to internal battles. Look at what they do on a daily basis:

- *Successful people say "yes" to their dreams and "no" to distractions.*
- *Successful people are guided by their focus and not by their feelings.*
- *Successful people remember their vision for life and ignore day-to-day vicissitudes.*
- *Successful people know the price of success is discipline . . . on a daily basis.*

DREAMS AND FOCUS: THE ULTIMATE COMBINATION

In our minds, internal conflict occurs when we have mixed emotions or conflicting thoughts about a decision we need to make. This is commonly known as cognitive dissonance—and we experience these conflicts thousands of times each day. Most of them are very minor; we resolve them so swiftly that they barely register with our conscious minds. Others are so monumental that it may take us hours, days, or months to resolve the conflict and make the decision. Between these two extremes are the little decisions of daily life—a continuum that looks like this:

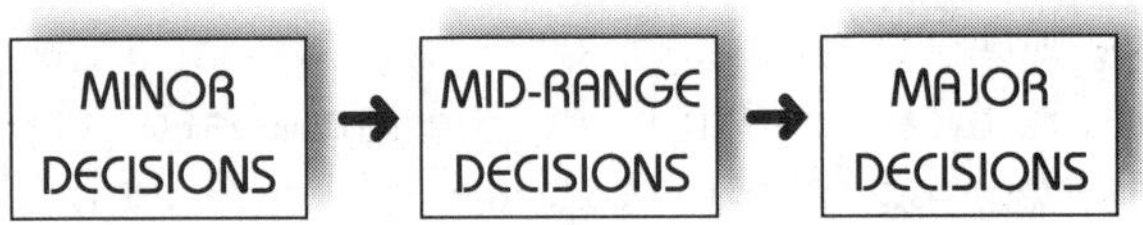

While this continuum appears simple, the process of making a decision is one of the most miraculous, high speed, and complex processes known to humans. It involves biochemistry, electrical impulses, physiological and emotional states, memory, myths, perceptions, and values. It makes our fastest computers look remarkably simplistic and slow.

Most of our daily business decisions fall in the "mid-range" of the decision continuum. We may think for a few seconds about whether or not we will check messages, make some calls, or go to a meeting, but we know that each of these simple decisions is not monumental. As stand-alone decisions, they are of little consequence. They are not life-and-death decisions. However, what many people miss is that success is *rarely* the result of a single major decision. Success is often the byproduct of countless *minor* decisions we successfully make on a daily basis. It's the *cumulative* effect of these daily decisions that yields success.

Having a clear dream makes it easier to make good decisions day by day. Have you ever been in a group of people trying to decide what restaurant to eat in or what movie to go see? Waiting for a group to reach a consensus of opinion can wear you out. Did you ever notice how the decision is made in the end? It is usually determined in one of the three following ways: By the person who speaks the *loudest* ("the squeaky wheel gets the grease"), by the person who speaks with the most *authority*, or by the person who speaks with the most *wisdom*. One of these opinions will almost always become the prevailing voice and determine the final vote.

This same kind of dialogue occurs within your mind when you have to decide if you are going to stay on task with business activities you know will cumulatively produce the results you want. The more clear and vivid your

> ***"Successful people are guided by their focus, not by their feelings."***

dream is, the more swiftly it "speaks up" with authority, wisdom, and a voice that demands to be heard.

Let's pretend we can listen in on the conversation that occurs in your mind after you have the thought, "Oh, I need to check my messages." The multiple internal opinions attempting to be heard may sound like this:

- The body says, "I'm tired. I'll just check my messages tomorrow."
- The emotions suggest, "I know I should check my messages but I don't want to. I'm sick of talking to

people. I don't feel like checking my messages now. I'll wait."

- The brain chimes in, "I'm exhausted. I don't have the energy to think or hear about another problem."
- The will gets caught up in the "group think" of the first three opinions expressed and capitulates by saying, "Good idea. Who cares. Let's take the rest of the day off."

At this point, the decision is made—case closed. There is no counter-opinion offered in the dialogue of the mind. The quick group consensus makes it easy to decide to ignore the task, and it helps to squelch the less prominent thoughts or feelings of doubt.

However, if a clear dream is also an integral part of this internal conversation, something else can happen that leads the discussion in a completely different direction. While hearing all the other opinions expressed, the dream speaks up and says:

> I know that I am tired and I don't feel like checking messages. I don't care to hear another problem and I would love to take the rest of the day off. *But*, if I want my dream of the future to come true, I have to stay on task. My future success is inevitable if I will sustain my daily focus. I would be a nut to let financial freedom in the future slip away because I was too lazy to push myself for a few more minutes today. Besides, if I will work just a little longer, I will have the satisfaction of getting done what I needed to while working toward my life goals for one more day. And there will still be some time later for me to rest. I need to remember that successful people are led by the power of their dreams while unsuccessful people are led by nothing more than their immediate desires. I need to remember what all suc-

cessful entrepreneurs instinctively know: Personal focus comes *before* personal financial freedom.

This is why dreams and aspirations need to be kept in the forefront of our minds. Vivid dreams help successful people make wise decisions; a clear vision of the future is what facilitates focus on a daily and hourly basis. This is why focus and dreams are the ultimate combination. If dreams are the rocket fuel of success then focus is the navigational system. One provides the energy and the other provides purposeful guidance. Focus takes the raw power of a dream and directs it toward victory. When focus is counterpart to our dreams, there is almost no limit to what we can accomplish.

"Focus takes the raw power of a dream and directs it toward victory."

By the way, the next time you notice someone exiting our industry as quickly as they entered it, be careful to properly interpret this phenomenon. Someone signing up and then doing nothing with the business is *not* necessarily a reflection on network marketing—it is a reflection on human behavior. Ours is an industry in which this endemic behavior can easily manifest itself, but it is not the *cause* of the behavior. Some individuals look at the attrition rate within the industry and *incorrectly* conclude that it reveals an inherent flaw in the business. This is not so. In actuality, it is statistical data that exposes the average person's inability to sustain focus in any endeavor.

HELLO? CAN YOU HEAR ME?

One of the curious aspects of being an author is that you are never sure what parts of your writing will connect most powerfully with your audience. Nor can you be sure if you are getting through to them on the concepts you most want them to comprehend. It's similar to those moments when you are on the phone speaking with someone and suddenly wonder if you have lost your connection. You find yourself saying things like, "Hello? Can you hear me? Are you still there?" This is what I feel at this point in the book. I am wondering if you can hear me and sense my desire for you to understand the vital role of focus in your success.

I spent several years coaching my daughters' soccer teams. I recall our first practice one year when the girls on the team were all about ten years old. My friend John and I had coached these girls the previous year so we were familiar with all of them and how well they played soccer. At the end of our first practice, he and I both gave our inspirational talks to get the girls focused for success. We told the girls how glad we were to be coaching them, how much we believed in them, and what we expected from them. We got on a roll and never doubted the compelling impact of our speech. We were sure the girls were inspired to dig deep, give maximum effort, and prepare to win the championship. Vince Lombardi would have been proud of our inspiring words.

When we were finished, the girls must have all been spellbound. No one said a word. They just stared at us, undoubtedly trying to take in the full import of what we had conveyed so eloquently. Finally, one girl dared to break the silence of this hushed and holy moment. She raised her hand and asked, “What color will our uniforms be?” John and I just looked at each other and fell over laughing. Maybe we had not communicated as effectively as we thought.

I hope that’s not the case here and that what I’ve been writing really does sink in. Take ownership of your dream, your vision, your future, and your life. Then take ownership of whatever it’s going to take to make it happen. Your future and your finances are your responsibility, and they turn on one rare quality: focus. Remember:

"Personal focus comes before personal financial freedom."

In the next chapter, we will learn how to take this concept and apply it directly to your business.

CHAPTER
THREE

15 MINUTES TO FINANCIAL FREEDOM

Think back for a moment to when you were a teenager in high school. How far into the future could you see on an average day? Was it 20 years? Ten years? Five years? How about five days? Let's face it, most of us could not see past the *weekend* at that age. We thought life planning meant determining what we were going to do on Friday and Saturday nights. On our best days, we looked into the future and envisioned the day when we would get our driver's license, go to a big dance, play in the big game, or graduate. Anything beyond this was so far into the distant future it seemed of no consequence. We lived in what is called the "immediate present."

Teenagers' inability to see how today's behaviors impact the next stage of life is what makes parenting them

such a fascinating challenge. Most teenagers cannot see the correlation between today and tomorrow. Parents, on the other hand, when it comes to their children, can clearly see the connection between current behavior and future success. They see how decisions or behaviors in one stage of life can hinder or enhance preparation for the next. When it comes to their children, parents understand what many teenagers do not:

The present impacts the future.

Today influences tomorrow.

The stages of life are connected to each other.

Successful entrepreneurs bring this same understanding to their businesses. They know today's actions determine tomorrow's outcomes. They live purposefully in the present because they know it will positively shape their future. They know the groundwork for success is developed in stages connected to one another. They constantly keep their future dreams connected to the focus of their daily lives.

Let's look at the different stages of life that parents see for their children. Parents know that a child's performance in high school has a direct bearing on the quality of college he or she will be admitted to. They also see how doing well in college determines what quality of occupation and salary level will be available upon graduation. This, in turn, will influence the quality of life their child enjoys. These sequential stages follow one another as shown below:

In the above continuum, parents are able to "begin with the end in mind." They can readily see how the performance of a child in high school sets in motion a quality of life for decades to come. What drives them crazy is when their children cannot seem to grasp the connection. This is the same thing that drives leaders in network marketing crazy. They see what their downline does not: that sustained focus and hard work for a season can set someone free for a lifetime.

There is nothing complicated about the above continuum. It is a simple, forward-moving, linear progression. You can easily see the logic and flow of it. Now, let's take this same simple concept and apply it to your business.

If someone on your team asked you how she could be ready to have extraordinary growth and success in her business one year from now, how would you answer? What would you tell her that would honestly position her for success? What advice would you offer that was substantive, practical, doable, and duplicable?

I suggest you tell her that if she wants next year to be spectacular, then she needs to understand that only the actions of *this* year can position her for that success. Help her to connect her present behavior to whether she'll get what she desires in the future. Like a parent with a teenager, help her to grasp the simple linear progression of success: To be positioned for great success *next* year, we need to make sure that *this* year is a good one. This leads us to a series of logical questions with self-evident answers that help to clarify this point:

Question: How do I have a great year in my business?

Answer: *You need to have a great quarter.*

Question: How do I have a great quarter in my business?

Answer: *You need to have a great month.*

Question: How do I have a great month in my business?

Answer: *You need to have a great week.*

Question: How do I have a great week in my business?

Answer: *You need to have a great day.*

Wondering how you can have a great *day* in your business is the ultimate question. It is the pivotal point on which everything else turns. When you can answer this, you have found the key that will put everything else in motion. It is the starting point that determines the end point. Knowing what makes a great day possible lets you know what it takes to have a great week, month, quarter, and year. When you can answer this question and take action, your life, business, and team will never be the same.

Successful people take the question one step further still: "How do I have a great *day* in my business?" The answer? *Focus for 15 minutes*. These 15 minutes of focus are simultaneously the most important and, for many, the least desirable part of the week, but knowing how the immediate present impacts the future, successful people don't let the momentary discomfort hold them back. They are not fenced in by the desire to avoid what is uncomfortable.

Before we go on to discuss just *how* you can build your business in 15 focused minutes, let's understand the urge to avoid them.

Don't Fence Me In

My in-laws live in a rural area near a busy highway. They love pets, but because of the highway near their home, a passing car or truck has hit almost every dog they have owned. After 20 years of this, their backyard is becoming a pet cemetery. Not long ago, my father-in-law (Grampa) bought another dog. It is a dachshund, one of those little dogs that look like a sausage. Because his legs are so short, he is unable to run very fast, so Grampa decided to name him "Pokey."

Soon after arriving, Pokey began to do what all the other dogs did—chase after every other dog chasing cars down the highway. Finally, in an effort to keep Pokey alive, Grampa installed an invisible electric fence around the perimeter of his five-acre yard. The day it was put in, Pokey thought it was just another day. When a dog came running along the highway, he was happy to go join it. However, just before he got to the edge of the yard, the mild electric shock from the fence zapped him. Pokey was startled and stopped dead in his tracks. He had no clue what had happened, but he did know that he didn't like it.

Not being the smartest creature in the world, Pokey quickly forgot about what happened. Later that morning, another dog came down the highway and Pokey went into high gear trying to join it. Once again, as he reached the edge of the yard he got zapped and quickly lost interest in joining the other dog.

Eventually, Pokey lost interest in running after every dog rambling along the road. He decided to avoid the discomfort rather than chase what he desired. He stopped chasing dreams and following his heart. He now believes that life beyond the edge of his known world is too uncomfortable. It is not safe or smart to go beyond the perimeter of his small world.

Pokey doesn't know it, but he has been duped! If he would be willing to endure just a *brief* moment of discomfort he would be able to run, roam, and do as he pleased. Pokey has traded a life of freedom for a moment of avoidance.

Of course, the fact that Pokey has been duped is no big deal. In his case, it may keep him alive. But when human beings get duped as Pokey has, it *is* a big deal. Giving up freedom to avoid discomfort is a dumb trade—a poor investment and a bad decision. And there are many people in the world of network marketing who are inches away from greatness and seconds short of freedom without knowing it. They only need to accept that everything they want is on the opposite side of an invisible electric fence called "brief discomfort."

The drawing below applies to Pokey as well as people:

Many people want to be financially free in the future, but they want to enjoy massive success without ever experiencing brief discomfort. They hope to remain in their safe, limited world and, at the same time, have unlimited freedom and success.

Successful individuals instinctively agree with Emory Austin when she says, "The comfort zone is the deadly zone." They don't want to be trapped in this zone; they want to bust through it!

True entrepreneurs understand:

- *You cannot have your desired future if you insist on remaining in your known present.*
- *You cannot capture success until you release yourself from being a captive of fear.*
- *You cannot taste freedom if you insist on avoiding discomfort.*
- *You cannot have new things until you start doing some new things.*

If you and your team will cross through the fence of "brief discomfort" for 15 minutes, it will change your business and your future by setting in motion a series of events that inevitably results in success.

YOUR FOCUSED 15 MINUTES

What does it mean to have a "focused 15 minutes"? A focused 15 minutes is a preplanned time specifically set aside to make contact with three groups of people: your downline, your customers, and your prospects. Each call has a specific purpose and should last only one minute. (If you are just beginning your business and do not yet have three people in your downline, you just saved three minutes!)

Here is what a focused 15 minutes looks like: Recognizing that you cannot have a great week without having some great days, you decide to do what is required to insure that this occurs. Let's say that you decide to set 15 minutes aside on Sunday evening to put your week in motion. When the time comes, you already know who you are going to call, you already have their phone numbers written down, and you know why you are calling them.

These 15 minutes of focus are preplanned because we *all* know how easy it is to spend time getting ready to do a task instead of *actually performing* the task. We can spend 15 minutes just looking for phone numbers, practicing what we are going to say, having the spontaneous urge to straighten up our work area, deciding to get a cup of coffee, etc. All of these delay tactics give us the illusion of working without requiring us to go through the invisible electric fence of discomfort. They create make-believe motion. In the end, they are completely unproductive and unprofitable.

How do you get started? What do you actually do or say when you make calls for 15 minutes? I recommend that you first call three people in your downline, then call three customers, and lastly, call three prospects.

Phoning Three People in Your Downline

When phoning your downline, I recommend you say something like the following:

> Hi, ______, I only have a moment, but I wanted to call and tell you three things: I believe in you. I believe in our business. And I am working my business right now for a focused 15 minutes.

What can you accomplish in this brief statement? In a few seconds, you are affirming the individual, sharing your positive belief in your business, and modeling to them that you are working your business *right now.*

When you make this call, do not let yourself get sidetracked asking or answering questions. This is not a time to chat, have "warm fuzzies," or get engrossed in discussion of any kind. The call should literally not last more than a minute. If the individual you contact wants to ask questions, you need to say, "I will be happy to answer your questions at another time, but I can't right now. I am working my business for a *focused 15 minutes*. I have three customers and three prospects to call. Feel free to call me tomorrow and I will be happy to answer your questions. For now, I called only to tell you that I believe in you, our business, and I am working our business right now."

Does this brevity and directness seem too blunt to you? Actually, being this direct is modeling focus, leadership, passion, and setting boundaries to those in your downline. It will work for you, not against you.

Phoning Three Customers

When contacting your customers, you might say:

> Hello, ______________ this is _______________. I know that I interrupted you so I am going to be very brief. Do you have 30 seconds? Good. I just called to tell you that I appreciate your business and that I am glad you are my customer. It is people like you who make my business both fun and profitable. If you need anything, please don't hesitate to contact me, but for now, I just want you to know that you and your business are appreciated.

What do you accomplish in *this* brief call? In a few seconds and sentences, you have expressed appreciation for your customer, let her know you are available if she needs anything, and shared your enthusiasm for your business. All of this builds your customer's loyalty to you and your business.

There are two reasons to be very brief in this call. First, you are attempting to limit each of your calls to one minute for maximum result in minimum time. Second, you have interrupted this customer with your unexpected phone call. She is hoping you will be very brief. Your brevity will be welcomed more than an uninvited call that lasts ten or 20 minutes—and your future calls will also be more readily received.

By the way, if you are calling a customer to express appreciation, don't contaminate the call by turning it into a "sales call" to tell them about new products or services. It will make the appreciation you express appear insincere. If you want to call a customer to inform them about new products or services this is okay, but may I suggest that when you do this, don't tell them that you called to express appreciation. Tell them you called to let them know about what is newly available, and then ask when it would be convenient to briefly tell them more. Schedule an appointment and get off the phone.

Phoning Three Prospects

The most important calls you will make are those to three prospects. These are the calls that give you appointments during the week, keep your business growing, and create new revenue. Most people avoid them because they are the least comfortable, but remember these calls have only two objectives: Discover the prospect's level of interest, and if it is adequate, set up an appointment to explain your business.

The next two chapters are devoted to how you can get prospects to *want* to meet with you and learn more about your business when you phone them. For now, let's discuss why this 15-minute commitment to focus is so powerful.

WHY IS A FOCUSED 15 MINUTES SO POWERFUL?

Initially, it is easy to overlook the power of a group of people focusing for 15 minutes. (For those who are just beginning their network marketing business or only working their business on a part time basis, I recommend 15 minutes once per week. For those who are full time, I recommend 15minutes each day.) Here are some immediate benefits:

- Fifteen minutes is a manageable amount of time. Most people can imagine going through the invisible fence of discomfort for 15 minutes, but if they need to stay out of their known comfort zone for much longer than this, they begin to avoid the time altogether. Would you rather have a team of people *actually phoning* their downline, customers, and prospects for 15 minutes each week, or a group of people that talks of spending an hour calling but never does?
- For most network marketers, getting the appointment creates more anxiety than going to the appointment. Having a preplanned time that is focused, brief, and effective keeps people willing to do it repeatedly.
- Knowing that others on your team are implementing a focused 15 minutes creates cohesiveness and mutual commitment within a team.

- When you and your team begin to duplicate this very simple system of focus, it will result in depth, growth, and residual income at an exponential rate. For example, if you called three prospects each week and got one appointment per week, you would have four appointments per month. What if one out of every four people joined your team and they too began to implement this process? How many people do you think would be on your team at the end of 12 months if this system perfectly reproduced itself? The answer is 4,096. Would this make a difference in your revenue and how fast you achieve your dreams?
- What would it mean to your company if every Sunday, ten thousand affiliates were on the phone to encourage their downline, thank customers, and phone prospects for appointments? What would it mean to you if every Sunday you had 50 people in your organization who were phoning their downlines, customers, and prospects?

All Dressed Up and No Place To Go

I respect the kind of income people earn in our industry, and I take pleasure in hearing the sales figures that networking organizations produce. But do you know what statistics I would enjoy hearing more than knowing how much money is being earned? I would love to know how much money was *not* made in our industry... all for want of a phone call that was never made. I have no doubt we have lost more revenue than has been made because countless people "never quite got around" to making a call that could have busted their business wide open. Successful people know that initiating a phone call is what kick-starts a chain of events that ultimately result in success, revenue, and freedom.

Most of Delta Airlines' planes have phones installed in each row of seats; on the digital screen of each phone appear the words, "How much will it cost not to call?" Interesting thought. This is the exact mindset of successful people in network marketing. They think of what it might cost them *not to call* rather than dwelling on whether or not they feel like calling.

You have probably heard the expression, "all dressed up and no place to go." This represents what some participants in our industry look like. They are in the business, want to see it grow, and faithfully attend meetings, but they never seem to have consistent appointments with new prospects. For various reasons, instead of taking the initiative and picking up the phone, they are sitting around like the Maytag repairman, waiting for their phone to ring. That's like waiting for Haley's Comet.

Entrepreneurs who begin with the end in mind and remember how the present impacts the future can easily see the power of staying focused for 15 minutes. A simple and consistent 15 minutes of focus results in weeks filled with meaningful appointments, which become months and quarters and ultimately a great year that will yield an awesome quality of life.

The next time you see leaders in your company enjoying recognition for achievement, ask yourself what inglorious moments they probably endured to get to the great moments. Public or professional success is usually earned in private where there is no audience, no applause, no approval, and no affirmation—just a single dream chased with private determination in the high speed of daily life. In network marketing, you can chase *and* capture that dream 15 minutes at a time.

CHAPTER
FOUR

HOW TO GET HOT RESPONSES FROM YOUR WARM MARKET

PART ONE

If you ask successful entrepreneurs about their early days in business, they'll almost always shake their heads and laugh at how little they knew what they were doing back then. Most of them will freely admit that they were long on vision and short on skill. They will chuckle at their naïve mistakes. If you ask them to grade their early performance, they will give themselves an "A" for effort and an "F" for knowledge. In retrospect, they realize that they began with high motivation, good vision, and minimal skills.

So how did they become successful? Over time, their skills became as strong as their motivation and vision

and success became inevitable. Their skills were producing the *results* that their minds had envisioned.

This same pattern is also true in network marketing. People who are long on vision and short on skill regularly jump in. But, like all other successful entrepreneurs, participants need to make sure their skills are growing while they protect their vision and motivation.

Let's Make a Deal

Skills are especially important when you talk to people in your warm market. Knowing *what* to say, *when* to say it, and *how* to say it is an invaluable skill. We will learn these skills in this chapter and the next, but first we have to come to an agreement. I need to know if you are willing to bring a light heart to these chapters. Is it okay with you if we have some fun looking at the common mistakes we all make in our industry? Can we be secure enough to admit our sincere but naïve mistakes? Is it all right if we laugh at ourselves while learning at the same time?

If you are game, then let's have some fun and learn how to get hot responses out of our warm markets. By the way, I have personally made every one of the mistakes I will point out, and I still make some of them on occasion as I continue to learn and develop my skills. If I can, I'd like to shorten your learning curve and teach you the skills I wish someone had taught me in the early stages of my business.

We Love You, But...

Like many teenagers, my daughters have the walls of their bedrooms covered with pictures and posters. I saw a new greeting card on the wall the other day. It is a drawing of a pastor standing in the pulpit giving a sermon. In large print it says, "Jesus loves you." Then, in small print it says, "But all your friends think you are a jerk!"

I love the card, but it reminds me of how some people in network marketing are viewed by family and friends. They could draw a greeting card that says, "We love you. But when you start talking about your business, you become a jerk." How do we avoid this? How do we get to the place where our goal is to talk about our business and the listener's goal is to hear more about our business? We can start by learning:

- How to start a fire.
- How to measure interest.
- How to pace our conversations.

How to Start a Fire in the Woods

If someone in your downline mentioned he was going camping in a remote wilderness area and asked you to teach him how to start a fire in the woods, what would you say? After a little thought, you would probably tell him that building a roaring fire in the wilderness is relatively easy... if you know the proper steps involved:

1. Make sure you have some matches.
2. Ignite a small pile of kindling using dry grass, moss, or wood chips.
3. Add small twigs not much thicker than a toothpick.
4. Gently lay several dry sticks about the thickness of a pencil across the fire.
5. Begin to lay sticks about one or two inches in diameter across the fire.

6. Begin to place logs as big as your arm on the fire.
7. Once the fire has a good base and is burning easily, gently place a log as thick as a telephone pole onto the fire.

By following the above sequence, the spark of a match can turn into a roaring blaze.

In network marketing, there are many people who feel as if they are in the wilderness trying to learn how to start a fire. They want to know how to take a spark of interest in a prospect and turn it into a roaring blaze.

"...take a prospect's spark of interest and help it grow into a blaze of curiosity."

When you teach people how to do this, their business and yours will catch like a wildfire.

Glance at the above sequence again and notice how we start very small and then progressively work our way up to the "big timber." In the beginning, the flames are very fragile and require careful treatment. The problem that most people have in starting a fire is that they get too impatient. In their eagerness to have a big fire, they prematurely use logs that are far too big to catch the flame.

The same mistake occurs every day in our industry. We forget to patiently take a prospect's spark of interest and help it grow, step by step, into a blaze of curiosity, eagerness, or excitement. Instead, we attempt to hurry the process, say too much too soon, and load the person down with information, facts, and figures prematurely. In the process, we extinguish the very flame we are trying to ignite.

If you saw someone trying to start a fire by dropping a 40-pound log on top of a small pile of barely burning grass, you would think they were silly—but this is exactly what we do in our business! We see a tiny spark of interest and then we dump the equivalent of 40 pounds of enthusiasm, information, and materials on top of it. The fire goes out immediately.

When this happens, some people in network marketing conclude one of two things: either our prospect "didn't get it," or it proves that this is a difficult business. It never occurs to them to question their own skills and techniques or find out whether or not they might be hindering their own success. When we learn how to "start a fire," we will discover that our business is not nearly as difficult as we thought. It is fun, rewarding, and actually rather easy when we know what we are doing. One of the skills that makes our business easier is learning to recognize the different types and levels of people's interest.

Types and Levels of Interest

Have you ever casually asked an acquaintance how he's doing and then find yourself stuck listening to every little detail of the last month? In your mind, you think, "Gee, I was just making casual conversation. I didn't expect a complete narrative!" You make a mental note to avoid asking this person how he is the next time you see him. It is the old saying, "Fool me once, shame on you. Fool me twice, shame on me."

We make the same mistake in our industry. People ask us a casual question about our business and we respond with far more information than they ever wanted. In the end, they are sorry they asked and make a mental note to avoid asking us about it in the future. To prevent this from happening, it helps to understand the various degrees of interest a prospect may have. To gauge a prospect's level of interest, it helps to classify interest into three categories—acute, moderate, and marginal—and measure it on a continuum of 0-10:

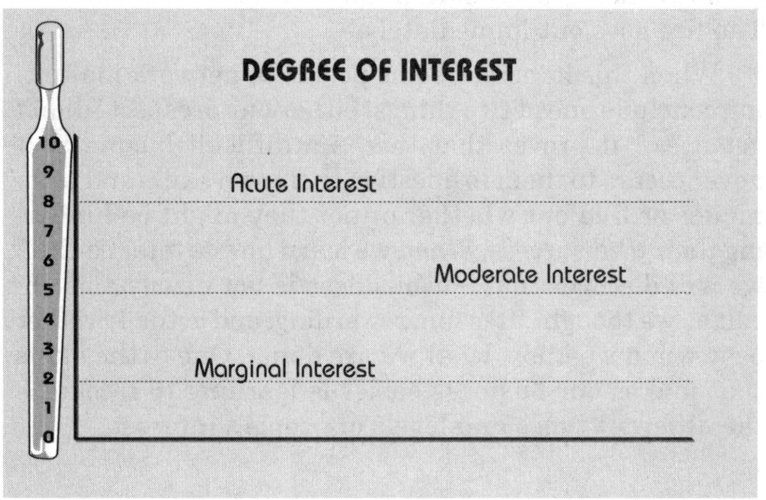

When you talk to prospects about your business, where do you think most of them rank on this continuum of interest? Occasionally, we meet someone who is acutely interested. They hear what we are doing and respond with, "This is exactly what I have been looking for! Can I sign up today?" Unfortunately this response comes about once in four life times. Others, on occasion, are moderately interested. They are genuinely curious about our industry, they are open-minded, positive, and want to learn more.

Over 90 percent of prospects, however, will have an interest that initially is marginal at best. On our scale of interest, they are between 1 and 3, and most of them are closer to the 1! When we understand this reality, it allows us to pace our conversation to *their* interest level—instead of our own.

> ***"Many of us confuse level one interest with level ten interest."***

To help you remember to do this, be sure to keep in mind the various ways that people exhibit marginal interest:

TYPES OF MARGINAL INTEREST

- friendly interest
- social interest
- minimal interest
- passing interest
- polite interest
- conversational interest
- brief interest
- casual interest

Note that all of the above types of interest would fall at level 3 or below on the interest scale. When prospects have marginal interest, all they have is "a spark." Our challenge is to take this spark and turn it into a hot fire. Many of us confuse level 1 interest with level 10. We see a brief flicker of interest and respond as if the prospect showed a blazing desire to hear more. Graphically, it looks like this:

Prospect's Level:	**Our Response Levels:**		
Of Interest	Enthusiasm	Information	Material
10	10•	10	10
9	9	9•	9•
8	8	8	8
7	7	7	7
6	6	6	6
5	5	5	5
4	4	4	4
3•	3	3	3
2	2	2	2
1	1	1	1
0	0	0	0

We often see a marginal level of interest in a prospect and react as if it were acute interest. We proceed to overwhelm the person with level 10 enthusiasm, far more information about our company, products, or services than the interest warranted, and then top it off with a truckload of tapes, videos, articles, books, or website addresses.

When we over-respond to prospects' interest, *they* are sorry that the conversation ever got started and *we* are sorry that it ends. In the future, we will be at cross-purposes. Their goal will be to avoid discussing our business while our goal will be to seek opportunities for such discussion. This is very different from interacting with prospects in such a way that they are eager to hear more about what we are doing, how it works, and how it relates to what *they want out of life*. One approach leads to avoidance, the other to anticipation.

To increase the likelihood that someone will want to hear more about your business, remember to bring the art of pacing into your conversations with others.

Pacing: The Forgotten Skill in Network Marketing

Any distance runner knows the need for pacing. Jockeys learn to pace their horses. NASCAR drivers constantly pace themselves with the competition and track conditions, along with their fuel supply and tire wear. In dating relationships and romance, pacing is an art. Lives hang in the balance when clinicians and surgeons do critical work for which pacing is vital. In negotiating business deals, pacing is an invaluable skill. Saying too much too soon, or too little too late, has broken many business deals that otherwise would have succeeded.

One of the biggest problems we have in our industry is that we get so excited about our message and are so in love with our business that we lose all sense of timing and pacing. We abandon many of our personal and professional skills when we begin to talk about our business. We think our business is so extraordinary that the normal rules of social and professional etiquette can be suspended. Our problem is that when we start talking about our business, we get weird! We morph into totally different people! We look like zealots trying to convert all of our family and friends.

Without question, our over-the-top excitement stirs desire in others—it stirs the desire to run! We make it impossible for them to listen to our message. They don't see financial freedom, they see a fanatic. They don't see wealth, they see weirdness. The only opportunity it makes them seek is the opportunity to change the subject or get away from us.

Keep in mind that I love enthusiasm. If you have ever heard me speak, you know there is no shortage of enthusiasm within me, and you *should* be unbelievably excited about our industry and your business. I am suggesting, though, that when we talk to prospects, our enthusiasm needs a regulator. It needs to be monitored and paced to the person with whom we are interacting.

Teenagers: The Best Examples of Pacing

If you want a refresher course in the art of pacing, don't bother going to a seminar. Don't pay a dime to learn this skill. Instead, to see the art of pacing in action, observe teenagers asking their parents for something they know may not be granted. They pay close attention to what they say, the best time to say it, and the best way to say it. Nothing is taken for granted.

For example, observe teenagers ask their parents if they can borrow the car or stay out later than usual. They don't barge in and just blurt out their request. They are much savvier than that. They study mom and dad's mood. If the parents appear stressed, they hold back. If the parents are irritable, they say nothing. If they seem tired and crabby, the teens remain silent. But, when the parents look relaxed, in a good mood, and approachable, the teenagers come in and tactfully float out their request. As they speak, they continue to monitor mom and dad as their audience. The entire time, they pay close attention to word choice, the tone and volume of their voice, and their speed of speaking. We can learn a great deal from this masterful pacing.

How skillfully do *you* pace your prospecting conversations? How do you know when it is "time to stoke the fire?" This becomes much easier when you remember the three parts of speaking.

The Three Parts of Speaking: Message, Messenger, and Audience

I am a professional speaker. Don't ask me how you know when you are officially a "professional" speaker, because I have no idea! I only know that large corporations pay me ridiculous amounts of money to come and speak to their senior management or at their annual conventions. There is, however, one aspect of professional speaking that I am very clear about: the three parts of a speech.

THESE PARTS OF SPEECH ARE:

1. The Message
2. The Messenger
3. The Audience

Consider these three parts of giving a speech. Which one do you think is the most important for me to keep in mind when I am on stage? Do you think it is the *message* I am giving, myself as the *messenger*, or is it the *audience* I am speaking to?

Without a doubt, the answer is the *audience*. It is my primary focus when I am giving a talk of any kind. How do you get to the place where you give a speech and focus on the audience above all else? You have to do two things. First, you need to know your speaking material so well that you are not worrying about what you are going to say. You only need to glance at your notes as a general guideline. Second, as a speaker you need to suspend concern about yourself during any speech. For example, I cannot worry about the audience noticing that I have lost much of my hair, or wonder if they like my suit, tie, or anything else about me. All of these concerns need to be abandoned during a speech so that I am free to focus on only one thing: the audience.

"Failing to study our audience is the most common mistake."

The great thing about being able to concentrate primarily on the audience is that they will tell you how you are doing. They will let you know if they are interested, having fun, and enjoying themselves. They will tell you if you are hot or cold, hitting the mark, and worthy of their time. When speakers learn this, there is a quantum leap in their effectiveness. Unfortunately for the audience, most speakers never learned these three parts of a speech—even those who think they are "professionals." That is why most speeches and speakers are unbearably boring.

Now, let me ask you to consider something else... Do the three parts of giving a speech apply to you when you are sharing your business with a prospect? If they do, which part is most important for you to be effective in your business presentation? Is it the *message* about your great business, you as the *messenger,* or is it your *audience*?

In reality, the same answer that is true for me is also true for you. The problem that we have in network marketing is that we get so excited about our *message* that we forget all about our *audience*! It never dawns on us to study our prospects to see if they appear intrigued, interested, or just wondering how long we are going to babble on before they find a diplomatic way to escape!

How do your prospects let you know if they are interested? They do it with many little signals. For example, if they are interested, they will keep asking you questions. They will keep looking at you, nod their heads, or smile. Observe their body language. What does their posture tell you? Are they relaxed, bored, tired, excited, eager, hanging on your words? What do their eyes tell you? Are they wide with interest or barely open? Are they glued to you or are they glancing around? What does their voice tell you? Is it animated, filled with energy or excitement? Or, does it sound tired or disinterested?

Failing to study our audience is the most common mistake in network marketing. It is understandable that we do this because it is appropriate to be excited about our message, but, as we will see, it is still a very costly error.

Don't Corner People—Captivate Them

One night, while driving with my wife to a party, I remembered that a particular woman with a knack for "talking your ear off" would be there. She is one of those people who can somehow corner you at a party and then talk to you for an hour without ever pausing to take a breath. Once she gets started there is no tactful way to escape her. She can talk endlessly about her husband, children, and dog as if they are the most fascinating subjects in the universe.

"We get so excited about our message that we forget all about our audience."

I learned the hard way about this fascinating conversationalist at a previous party, so I told my wife, "Linda, there will be a woman at this party who will talk your ear off if you give her a chance. Once she gets going, there is no easy way to end a conversation with her. You will be trapped. My advice is that you don't even stop to say 'hello' to her. If she says something to you, answer her briefly but keep moving, because if you stop you will be stuck. If she does corner you, I want you to know that I will not come to rescue you. You are on your own, because I know what will happen when I come up to join the two of you. Immediately you will politely excuse yourself and say that you need to get something to drink. Then I will be left standing there! So if you get caught, you are on your own." She laughed and considered herself forewarned.

Do you know what is worse than being cornered by someone like this? It is realizing that the same things might be said of us when we get so excited about our business that we are sure everyone must hear about it whether they want to or not.

I wonder how often the family members of someone in network marketing have said something similar to what I shared with my wife. How many times has a friend or family member been driving in a car and said, "No matter what you do, please don't ask Larry about his new business! If you do, he will get so excited that he cannot shut up. He will talk on and on and on and you will be stuck with him all night."

To learn how to effectively pace our conversations with others, we can learn from former President George Bush.

Lessons from a President

Most people can rattle off a list of their most embarrassing moments. Usually, these moments seem dreadful when they occur but actually have no serious consequences. As time passes, these same moments are often remembered with a laugh and actually become a source of delight as we relive them.

If you were former President George Bush, what would you classify as your most embarrassing moment? My guess would be that this man, who has accomplished an extraordinary number of things in his lifetime, has one moment that stands out above all others. It would be when he, as the President of the United States, was attending a formal state dinner with Japan's Prime Minister, Kiichi Miyazawa. During the course of the dinner, President Bush had a food reaction and managed to (there is no delicate way to put this) barf all over the Prime Minister of Japan.

I can only imagine the expression on people's faces when this happened. What did the security people do? How about the other guests or staff? What would you do if you were the one serving the food? It is hard to imagine asking the guests if they were interested in any dessert. As a result of this event, the Japanese now have a verb for "losing your lunch." It is called *Bushusuru*.

How does this embarrassing moment of a former president relate to those of us in network marketing? We have the same problem with prospects that President Bush had with the Prime Minister of Japan: We keep barfing all over people! If there is one piece of advice some of us

STOP

"George Bushing" all over people!

need to remember, it is to *stop* "George Bushing" all over people! Our prospects only lose their appetite for hearing more. This is not the best strategy for getting a hot response out of our warm markets.

When I do live training with network marketing companies, someone inevitably asks, "Tom, what do I do if I have already George Bushed all over my entire warm market?" It is a great question that always brings a lot of understanding laughter. Fortunately, this problem is fixable.

If you (like I used to do) have George Bushed all over others, take a moment to understand what has happened.

In their eyes, we have lost some credibility. We do not look safe to talk with when it pertains to our business. They do not trust us in this area. Our task is to do a little damage repair and to redevelop trust and credibility. It is our job to demonstrate to these people that we have learned to talk about our business briefly and calmly while still being excited and confident.

Let me give you an example. Let's say that Larry is involved in network marketing and he has George Bushed all over his family and warm market. He has made every mistake imaginable: He talked too long, said too much, and he did not pay attention to his audience. Additionally, he got weird on people, far too excited, and repeatedly barfed all over anyone who gave him the slightest indication of interest. Consequently, everyone in Larry's family is gun-shy about asking him anything about his business—indeed, they avoid it at all costs.

Now let's imagine that there is a large family gathering and everyone is eating dinner. So far, everyone has successfully avoided asking Larry about his business. However, Sue, who is in from college, does not know that Larry "George Bushes" all over people at the slightest mention of his business. Unaware, she innocently says, "Larry, I understand that you are involved in a network marketing company or some sort of new business. What is it that you are doing? Do you like it?"

At this moment, the hearts of all the others around the table sink. Their worst fear has now materialized. Someone gave Larry an opening to start talking about his network marketing business. They begin to look at their watches and wonder if it would be permissible to leave the family gathering early even though only salad has been served.

If Larry wants to demonstrate that he has learned to be a little more balanced and normal, he can use one of two options:

Option 1: Larry can simply respond, "Sue, I am involved with a new business. I have never been more excited or convinced about anything I have ever done. Thanks for asking. How have you been doing?"

Option 2: Larry can respond with, "Thanks for asking. I am involved with a network marketing company and I love what I am doing. But to be honest with you, in the early stages of my business I was so excited about it that I talked everyone's ear off. I am finally learning to be brief. So let me just say that I have never been more sure of anything that I have ever done. Thanks for asking. How have you been lately, Sue?"

What is Larry doing in the above two responses? In the first option, Larry simply *demonstrates* to others that he is learning to be brief about his business. In the second response, Larry demonstrates that he can be brief *plus* he openly admits, in a lighthearted style, that in the past he made mistakes in his over-the-top enthusiasm. Additionally, in both responses, Larry takes the spotlight of attention and, instead of keeping it on himself and his business, quickly puts it back on Sue.

When Larry utilizes either of the above options, his listeners begin to sense that Larry is learning to be excited while managing his zeal. They sense that it is becoming possible to ask Larry about his business without him becoming weird and George Bushing all over his listeners. It is Larry's first step toward rebuilding trust, safety, and credibility with these people, and to solidify the difference, he will probably need to repeat this process several times before they actually come back to inquire more seriously about his business. When they do begin to inquire again, Larry will have to be wise in his responses or risk losing the very credibility he was recreating.

In the next chapter, we will see how, with the help of a few new ideas and skills, it can be easy to get people interested in learning more about your business.

CHAPTER
FIVE

HOW TO GET HOT RESPONSES FROM YOUR WARM MARKET

Part Two

Remember that we still have a deal in effect from the last chapter. We are giving ourselves permission to laugh at our sincere mistakes as a means of learning how to be more effective and successful. So, with your continued permission, let's have some fun while learning some invaluable insights and skills.

Have you ever used an Internet service that generates revenue through advertising? For example, America Online shows viewers a new ad every day when they access the Internet. Viewers respond to the ad by clicking their mouse on one of two boxes that say:

No Thanks TELL ME MORE!

With all of these ads, the advertiser has only a brief moment to create interest in viewers as they make a split-second decision to go one way or another.

Now imagine being on the Internet and having an ad pop up that you did not want to know more about. You click your mouse on "No thanks," but there is no response—in fact, the ad proceeds to give you the very information you said you were not interested in! At first you would be puzzled. Then you might begin to repeatedly click the mouse, moving it all over the "No thanks" box. Now imagine that this inability to exit the ad went on for 30, 40, or 50 minutes! There is no escaping it! By the end of this time, you might be banging on your mouse and yelling at your computer screen! You can almost hear Regis Philbin in the background asking you, "Is that your final answer?" each time you click "No thanks." Soon you would be hollering, "Of course that is my final answer, now let me out of here!"

Sound familiar? Too often, prospects are politely clicking the "No thanks" box only to have us keep on yakking. We need to honor their request. We will have other opportunities to share when they are ready to say, "Tell me more!" and the first step in getting that response is learning our *own* primary task.

Your Primary Responsibility

I don't know much about cars, but one thing I do know is that they all have a firewall built into them. The firewall is a physical barrier between the engine compartment and the passenger area built into the car to muffle noise from the engine, contain fires, and protect passengers in an accident.

"We want to draw people to our business like a magnet instead of repelling them away."

Similarly, there is also a “firewall” that separates every network marketing company’s main corporation (the engine) from the representatives of the company out in the field (the passenger area). This firewall is one of the best aspects of network marketing. It allows those who affiliate with a company to grow their own team without having to manage the myriad of internal issues that face any growing corporation. As long as the engine is running well, participants in the field can focus on learning how to drive the business.

Many people have been around network marketing for years and have never stopped to distinguish their role as representatives of the company from the corporation’s role. Naturally, network marketing is most effective when the corporation and representatives are each fulfilling their responsibilities. Here’s what should happen on each side of the firewall:

The Corporation's Responsibility	**The Representatives' Responsibility**
1. It is the corporation's responsibility to open new *markets*.	1. It is the representatives' responsibility to open their *mouths*.
2. It is the corporation's responsibility to find and develop new *products*.	2. It is the representatives' responsibility to find and develop new *people*.
3. It is the corporation's responsibility to open new *countries*.	3. It is the representatives' responsibility to open *conversations*.

If our primary task is to start conversations and find and develop new people, then we need to learn the art of interacting with people in such a way that they are eager to hear more about our business. We need to stir their hunger and curiosity. We want to draw people to our business like a magnet instead of repelling them away. The question is, what draws them?

Connect the Dots!

Have you ever heard the expression, "So what does that have to do with the price of eggs in China?" You might say this in a conversation if someone makes a statement that seems unrelated to what is being discussed. The comment seems irrelevant, like it came out of nowhere. This quip is a humorous way of saying that without a clear connection to the current conversation, you don't know what to do with what the person said.

This same "disconnect" can occur when network marketers begin to share their business with others. If you want to stir increasing interest in your listeners, then show how your business, story, and enthusiasm are relevant to *their* lives, not just yours. If you don't make this connection for your prospects, they are nothing more than passive listeners. They may briefly listen to your story as a friend (marginal interest), but they will quickly lose interest if you don't begin to connect your business to their situation. The longer you talk without helping them see how your business relates to their needs or desires, the more at risk you are that they'll think, "So what does this have to do with the price of eggs in China?" i.e. "What does this have to do with me?"

You'll get a completely different reaction, however, when you create this connection. A major shift will occur in how your prospects perceive what you're telling them.

THEY WILL START TO SEE YOUR BUSINESS AS...

- personally interesting to them
- relevant to their lives
- worth taking the time to learn about
- a solution to their problems
- an answer to their prayers
- a source of hope
- a practical strategy for their success

- an exit strategy for things they want to end
- a source of positive change in their lives
- good news!

Don't risk appearing intrusive and irrelevant. If you want to move people up the interest scale, from marginal to moderate to acute, begin by connecting your business to *their* lives. When you make the connection, it stirs the flame of interest, and if you continue to carefully build the fire, it will keep burning.

There are two other skills that make it very easy to relate your business to the lives of prospects. The first is to be aware that there are three general reasons why people get involved in our industry. The second is a listening skill that enables you to carefully observe the specific reasons a particular prospect would join you in your business.

What Would You Do With 40 Minutes?

Before looking at the next two skills, let me ask you to consider something. If you had 40 minutes with a prospect in your warm market, how much of that time would you use to present your business to them for the first time? Many of us would spend five minutes chatting and then 35 minutes eagerly explaining our business. Instead, may I suggest that you learn to spend 35 minutes *listening* to your prospect and only five minutes explaining how your business relates to what they want out of life.

Admittedly, the thought of this is anathema to some people in our industry. They see it as a waste of time. They would rather see if a spark of interest exists and then promptly test the strength of the spark by dropping a 40-pound log on it. To them, network marketing is simply a numbers game in which you churn through countless people looking for a few good ones.

My contention is that with our warm market, we have the time to carefully build the fire via creating interest, relevance, and credibility. Would you rather have 35 minutes that assure your prospects they have no need to speak with you again about your business, or five minutes that create a hunger in them to learn more about your business in the future? Making the wrong choice about how to use your time with a prospect is like nailing the doors of communication shut. Listening opens them widely so communication can continue.

Three Reasons Why People Get Involved

It is easy to assume that people get involved in network marketing for only one reason—money—but if we pay closer attention to our audience, we discover that most people are attracted to network marketing for one of *three* reasons: revenue, recognition, or affiliation.

> **Revenue**: This attraction is obvious. Network marketing gives people the opportunity to create an ongoing stream of residual income. But do not immediately assume this is the primary attraction for everyone. It isn't. Also, pay attention to your prospects to see what *amount* of revenue would be attractive to them. There are hundreds of thousands of people who got started

in this industry only wanting to make several hundred dollars per month. They were not after "big money." They got started with very modest, practical dreams.

Affiliation: Many people get involved in network marketing simply because they enjoy the social interaction of attending meetings and making new friends. They are relationship-driven, not revenue-driven, and in network marketing, they find a group of people who are generally very friendly and fun—people with a zest for life, invigorated by the joy of having a dream and a vehicle for achieving it. Network marketing is a great place for these people, and they are great for network marketing. They bring warmth, life, and humor wherever they go.

Recognition: This attraction is less obvious, but still very important. Many people get involved in network marketing because they sense that it is an industry in which people are publicly honored for their efforts. They see that participants are frequently recognized for hard work, being promoted, and for personal achievements.

When speaking with prospects, ask yourself, "Which of the three general reasons for involvement might be most important to them individually?" Don't assume that you know their reason, and avoid the common mistake of assuming that *your reason* for involvement must be the same as *theirs*. Pay attention to them as your audience and you will see their reason for joining you begin to emerge.

Lessons from an Old Man

I regularly spend time on Capitol Hill because I am an executive coach to members of Congress. A common ritual I've observed when it comes time for a vote is members rushing from their offices to the voting chamber in the Capitol with only 15 minutes to do so. To expedite their walk, a subway runs underground from the members' office buildings to the Capitol. This subway is a simple five-car train with two passenger cars in the front, one in the middle where the subway driver sits, and two more in the back. Each passenger car seats six people. The ride lasts only one minute.

When a vote takes place, all 435 members of Congress drop what they are doing and rush over to the Capitol. When this happens, the little subway train gets extremely crowded. It is not uncommon to jam ten or 12 people into each car.

> ***"People need to feel valued and appreciated for their talent, skill, and efforts."***

Not long ago, I was in the midst of a meeting with a committee chairman when a vote began. We hurried to the subway and jumped in. It was standing room only as all the members of Congress stood there in their power suits and ties. They looked very important, far too important to notice or talk to the driver of the subway, a sweet old man about 80 years of age. As we made our one-minute trip, I began to talk to him over the noise of the train and chatter of members. I asked how his day was going, what time he came in, if we were having many votes, and if he knew what time we would adjourn for the evening.

When the train arrived in the Capitol, its doors opened and I was ready to jump off the train and hurry to the vote with the chairman. Just before I got out, I felt a tug on my suit sleeve. I turned and realized it was the subway driver. He didn't say a word. He just looked at me and smiled. Then he reached into his pocket, pulled out two pieces of candy, and handed them to me.

Why did he do this? It was his way of saying, "thank you." Thank you for noticing me. Thank you for treating me like a human being. Thank you for not acting as if I am only a piece of the machinery. Thank you for not acting as if I am unworthy of being spoken to. Thank you for not treating me as if I am invisible.

I still have those two pieces of candy. They serve as a reminder of what that dear old man taught me: the power of giving recognition to others.

When Good Efforts Go Unnoticed

There are hundreds of thousands of people who give their very best efforts to their work, spouse, or children every day. They are doing as much as they can and the best that they can, but for many of them, the efforts go unnoticed or unappreciated.

- Ask someone what it is like to do extraordinary work only to have a boss take the credit for it. I just spoke with a bright young man who has been doing extremely creative research in the area of nuclear medicine. He had original ideas that no one understood. On his own time, he began to test his theories. He had no support, no backing, and no encouragement from his boss. Now that his research is getting national recognition, his boss is taking all of the credit. This brilliant young man does not care about making money, he only wants to make some contributions in the field of medicine, but he is so weary of a selfish and insecure boss taking credit for all of his breakthrough research, he is ready to quit. If he does, it is not only a loss to his corporation, it is a loss to humanity. This happens every day in the work world.

- Ask dedicated employees what it is like to be told that a project at work has to be given "top priority." They drop everything, work overtime and weekends, neglect their personal lives, and endure the additional stress and pressure. They complete the project only to be told that there has been a change of plans—what they did was not necessary after all. Their skill, efforts, and sacrifice all go unrecognized.
- Ask spouses or parents what it is like to give their finest efforts to their home life and never hear a "thank you." Ask what it is like to be reminded regularly of their shortcomings but rarely told of all the things they do well.

There is a legitimate human need for recognition. People need to feel valued and appreciated for their talent, skill, and efforts. Many individuals have found that good effort and hard work are recognized and honored in network marketing. They continue to work hard and be successful because they are glad to feel noticed, appreciated, and valued. They are not motivated by revenue. They are motivated by the power of legitimate recognition. This is one of the great strengths of our industry.

Learn to Listen in "3-D"

Do you know that people frequently tell you *directly* why they might like to join you in your business? They do—and repeatedly. The problem with many of us is that we don't hear it. Or we make the classic fatal mistake of getting so over-excited about their interest that we chase them away.

How do people tell us their reasons for wanting to join our team? They do it in ordinary conversations as they tell us about their lives. They don't come right out and say, "I need to join you in what you are doing," or "I need you to help me learn how to create some income." They are subtler than this; but when you learn to truly *listen* to your audience, you will discover that they are repeatedly telling you why they need to join you—loudly and clearly.

How do we learn to hear people telling us their reasons? By learning to "listen in 3-D."

LISTENING IN 3-D MEANS LEARNING TO LISTEN WHEN PEOPLE:

1. Tell us their *Dreams*
2. Tell us their *Desires*
3. Tell us their *Discontents*

What does this look like in daily life? It is not someone calling us up and saying, "I feel discontented today. Can you meet with me and tell me how your business relates to my life struggles?" As the saying goes, "In your dreams!" It looks more like the following two examples:

- While chatting on the phone with a friend, she shares some personal exasperation with you—"I can't believe it! Our dishwasher just broke and now we need to spend $300 on a new one. This is the last thing we can afford right now."
- While hanging out with a friend, he says, "We just got an $800 car repair bill. What we really need is a new car, but we can't afford one. In fact, we can't even afford this stupid repair bill."

If someone shared one of these two pieces of information with you, what would you do? Many of us would make one of two mistakes. Mistake number one is not even thinking about how to relate their comment to our business. Mistake number two is to suddenly get very animated and jump all over them about their need to look at our business, get involved, and make vast sums of money! In one case, we say too little; in the other, we say too much and get far too excited. Both mistakes result in our friend's problem not being solved and in our business stagnating.

How do you cultivate the skill of listening in 3-D? First, remember the power of focusing on prospects as your audience and listening carefully to what they say. You become very special to people when you listen to them and demonstrate that you understand what they are experiencing. This is true because people are not accustomed to being respectfully listened to and understood. As Ralph Waldo Emerson stated, "It is a luxury to be understood." Grant this "luxury" to others and you will be amazed at the time and respect you will receive from them when you relate your business to their lives.

By the way, I am not suggesting that you learn to listen to others as a ploy or as a means to an end. Listen because you care. Share your business with them because you understand their life situation, and because you know how your business personally relates to what they want or need. Keep in mind that there are few people more eloquent or interesting than a good listener. Maybe this is why the following anonymous poem was written:

His thoughts were slow
His words were few
And never formed to glisten.
But he was a joy to all his friends
You should have heard him listen!

When listening in 3-D, pay attention to the various ways individuals express their dreams, desires, and discontents. Let your mind be like a computer doing a word search for their pressures, wishes, regrets, goals, longings, hassles, frustrations, hopes, hobbies, interests, problems, struggles, worries, and fun.

LEARN TO LISTEN WHEN PEOPLE SHARE THINGS SUCH AS:

If money were no problem...

If I had my druthers...

If I could I would...

If I had the time...

If I were granted one wish...

While interacting with people in your warm market, learn to pay attention to the seasons and rhythms of life. Notice that:

- In September, you hear people speak of the cost of getting kids back to school—clothing, school activities, books, hobbies, sports, lessons, or tuition.
- In December, you hear people discussing the cost of the holidays—gifts, travel, parties, etc.
- In January, you hear people talk about bills coming in from the debt they incurred in December.
- In February and March, you hear people in the cold climates wishing they could get away for a warm vacation.
- In April, you hear people talk about needing money for taxes or wanting to buy new clothes for spring and summer.
- In the summer, you hear people discuss their desires for a long vacation, travel, or just time off.

If you listen carefully, you will discover that people are regularly giving you insights into the dreams, desires, and discontents of their worlds. When you learn to identify what they want, and then relate your business to their specific longings, you will see a quantum leap in their interest and appreciation for your business.

Find Your Voice

If you want to have maximum effectiveness in presenting your business, you need to "find your voice." Give yourself permission to be what I call an "ACE." What does this mean?

BEING AN ACE MEANS THAT YOU:

- Learn to speak with *Authority*.
- Learn to speak with *Conviction*.
- Learn to speak with *Enthusiasm*.

Consider these three different voices: authority, conviction, and enthusiasm. Which one of these do you think people in network marketing use most frequently? You know the answer—enthusiasm. In fact, for some people in our industry, enthusiasm is the *only* voice that they have ever learned to use. These people just "enthuse all over the place!" Their assumption is that prospects will get swept up in the force of their enthusiasm and immediately join their team.

I enjoy seeing enthusiasm in people. It is a fabulous quality and one of my favorite characteristics of our industry. But we also need to be aware of the value of learning to speak with conviction and authority. This is especially true when you are speaking to prospects who are more sophisticated when it comes to understanding business or finances.

Let me give you an illustration. If you and I were friends or acquaintances and you asked me to look at a business you were involved with, I might look at it. But your enthusiasm would have almost nothing to do with my decision to join you. I would be watching to see how much conviction and authority you have. This is what is most compelling, most powerful, and most influential in my response to you and your business. I want to know your level of belief and your reasons for believing in it. If these make sense to me, then I will begin to have some belief of my own. When I have belief of my own, it will result in my *own* enthusiasm for your business.

Don't worry if you have never learned to be an ACE. It is okay for you to still be learning to speak with authority and conviction. Many people have had wonderful success by beginning with nothing more than a voice of enthusiasm. But the fact that you began there does not mean you have to stay there. As your team and business grow, your ability to be an ACE will prove invaluable. And if you want more success in attracting seasoned veterans of the business and financial world to your team, then you need to give yourself permission to find your voice. You need to speak with authority, conviction, *and* enthusiasm.

Study the top leaders and income earners in your company. Get to know people like Jimmy Dick, Kathleen Deoul, Meda Branwell, and Allyn Jones. More often than not, you will discover that they bring a rich mixture of authority, conviction, and enthusiasm to their interaction with others. This skill may have been present within them prior to starting their network marketing business, or they may have found and developed it as their business grew. In either case, observe the impact of being an ACE when they interact with others.

Watch the Banner Announcements

Have you noticed the increasing use of banner announcements at the bottom of your television screen? They are particularly common on cable news shows like CNN. These allow you to watch the main program while glancing at the banner for other bits of information.

When you are speaking with people about your business, try imagining a banner announcement continually scrolling across the screen of your mind. This banner is your own private reminder of the skills we have been discussing. Following are the thoughts I suggest you load onto your mental banner. Let these thoughts be constant reminders of how to skillfully interact with others. People I have coached call them, "The Barrett Banner":

THE BARRETT BANNER

1. *I will see this person again.* (This thought reduces the urgency to tell them everything you know about your business.)
2. *I am just trying to start a fire.* (This thought reminds you to feed, not smother, the spark of interest in a listener.)
3. *There are various types of interest: acute, moderate, and marginal.* (Don't mistake level 1 interest for level 10.)
4. *The three parts of speaking are the message, the messenger, and the audience.*
5. *Stop "George Bushing" all over people!*
6. *People get involved for three reasons: revenue, recognition, and affiliation.*
7. *Listen in "3-D" for dreams, desires, and discontents.*
8. *Connect the dots.*
9. *Be an ACE. Speak with authority, conviction, and enthusiasm.*

May I suggest that you memorize all of the above points. They will help you recall some of the skills that are so profoundly determinative of the reaction you will evoke in your listeners. The more readily you, and those on your team, begin to apply these skills, the more you are going to get hot responses from your warm market.

Is It Really Necessary to Know All of These Things?

Some people may think that the above skills are too laborious to learn and implement. They can even name people who joined their business despite the "George Bush" technique. No doubt this does happen. My concern is not the few that get in using this method, but it is the thousands that "get away" because they were repelled by our style.

Recently I had dinner with one of the premiere surgeons in America and he began to share with me the many frustrations of managed care and how it has taken the joy out of his work. After listening carefully, I suggested that he consider looking at network marketing. His response was, "I would rather starve to death." I laughed, told him that he might, and then asked why he thought this. His response was that he had seen this business done so badly by so many people that he could not imagine affiliating himself with our industry.

I could only agree with him. Then I suggested he take a look at the new level of professionalism being brought into our industry. Fortunately, he trusts me enough to do this. But it will be slow starting his fire because of the countless others who approached him before me.

We have every reason to be proud and excited about our industry. Let's demonstrate this pride and excitement in such a way that others can't wait to join us. Let's all do our part to conduct business in such a way that people say eagerly, "Tell me more!"

CHAPTER
SIX

SO WHAT IF SOMEONE SAYS "NO"

The restaurant came with the highest recommendations. With a nationally known chef, it had a reputation for excellent food both prepared and presented with attention and care. Each year, it was rated among the top three restaurants in Chicago, so it was with great anticipation that Kathy and her five guests arrived and waited for their reserved table to become available.

After all were comfortably seated, a server appeared and welcomed them to the restaurant. He handed each a menu, walked them through the wine list, took their orders for drinks and appetizers, and, just before leaving, proudly explained the two specials the chef had meticulously prepared for the evening.

At the appropriate time, the server returned to take everyone's order for the main course. Each guest gave his and her menu selection. With each order, the server

became increasingly distressed. Kathy placed the final order, and as her guests had done, she declined the two specials the server had eagerly recommended and chose another appealing option.

As it happened, Kathy was not just the last to order—for the server, she was the last straw. He could contain his frustration no longer. With tears in his eyes, he looked at the guests and asked why none of them had ordered the chef's specials he had recommended. He told them they had been prepared with great care, looked and tasted wonderful, were fairly priced, and wanted to know why no one had listened to him. As they stared in stunned silence, the server threw his pen and order pad down on the table and proceeded to take off his formal jacket and throw it on the table as well. As drinks were spilling everywhere, he simply declared, "If nobody wants what I have to offer, then I quit!" He turned and walked out of the restaurant.

"If someone says 'no' it's not a big deal unless you make it one."

Can you imagine a server who is so over-identified with his job that he takes it as a personal rejection when guests decline his suggested entrée? Fortunately, this story is fictitious, but it does parallel the response of some people in network marketing when a prospect declines to get involved. They are over-identified with their business and feel personally rejected if someone chooses not to order their products or join their team. They are not sure how to respond after they eagerly presented their products, services, or business to someone who simply said, "no."

To remain confident and upbeat in network marketing, it helps to understand *why* some people decline your offers. It also helps to learn how to respond with *confidence* when this occurs.

Let's have some fun and learn to develop accurate responses to those moments when, for whatever reason, people are not interested in what you have to offer them. As the glib expression goes, let's "get a grip." So what if someone says "no"? It is not a big deal unless you make it one, and this only happens if you forget your task and the multiplicity of reasons that cause people to decline your invitation—none of which has anything to do with you or your business.

Sharing Your Business is Not as Simple as it May Seem

At first glance, telling someone about our industry seems a rather straightforward interaction. They will either "get it" or they won't. They will join us or they won't. It seems like a simple "yes" or "no" decision people need to make, and on the surface, this is the case. Keep in mind, though, that we are also connecting with people at a much deeper level.

Have you ever gone fishing with a bamboo pole? It is wonderfully simple. All you need to do is bait the hook, attach a sinker and a bobber, and throw the line into the water. The baited hook drops below the surface of the water, and then you just sit and wait. But how do you know when you have a fish on the line if you cannot see the hook below the water's surface?

If you have ever done this, you know the answer: you can see the bobber bouncing on the surface of the water. It is important to understand that the bobber is not where the action is—the real action takes place underwater at the hook level. The bobber is merely a surface indicator of something deeper going on that you cannot observe directly.

This is what working as an executive coach or doing clinical work is like—at the "bobber level," you see people's surface behavior, actions, and attitudes, but the real insight comes from paying attention to what is happening *below* the surface at the "hook level." This is the level at which the true meaning and motivations of human behavior originate. The most skilled clinicians and executive coaches are those who learn to look past the surface behaviors at the bobber level and astutely observe and interpret what is going on below the surface at the hook level.

Keep this in mind, because when you share your business with prospects, their surface reaction may be vastly different from their "hook level" reaction. There is almost always far more going on within them than you are able to observe. You should know that a simple business presentation may touch upon your listeners' most deeply held beliefs and assumptions—about their place in the world, their own abilities, or how others respond to them. Some of these beliefs will be negative, many personal. You won't realize you've touched on one, and they may not even be fully aware themselves, so when people tell you "no," don't concern yourself with *why*. All you need to do is not take it personally and move on. Don't attempt to analyze them or talk them into joining you. And *never* attempt to shame them for not joining you. Let it be—go on about your business with the next person.

There is a vast array of reasons why people will "pass" on the life-changing opportunity you offer. Some reasons are misguided, some legitimate, some silly, and some are just sad.

REASONS WHY SOME PEOPLE SAY "NO" TO THIS LIFE-CHANGING INDUSTRY

- They have no dream.
- They are already achieving their dream.
- They have no hope.
- They have no energy.
- They have no time.
- They already have enough time.

- They have no money.
- They have no financial need.
- They are not entrepreneurs.
- They are already entrepreneurs.
- They have no confidence.
- They think network marketing is below them.
- They don't understand leverage.
- They fear change.
- They already enjoy what they're doing.
- They fear failure.
- They fear success.
- They are already successful.
- They are lazy.
- They are risk-averse.
- They doubt anyone would take them seriously.
- They are anxious about what their family or friends would say.
- The timing is not right.
- They like you but do not want to do anything that makes them feel as if they are working *for* you.
- They view their past as the predictor of their future and, therefore, conclude they will never succeed in anything, including network marketing.

So when people don't say "yes" to you, just take it in stride. Don't try to persuade them. Don't attempt to find a deeper meaning for their lack of involvement. Keep your dream in mind, stay focused, and get ready for the next person with whom you will share your business.

By the way, if you inadvertently hit on a powerful, personal concern with prospects, do you think they are going to tell you this concern if they hardly know you? Of course not! They will protect their privacy and offer a general reason for why they will not participate. Many times they will raise an ostensible concern about your product/service, company, or industry. These are smokescreens to keep you, or even themselves, from facing the real "below the surface" reasons for their decision not to get involved. Let them have their privacy while you keep your private dreams intact.

Keep Your Perspective to Keep Your Joy

Having read this far into my book, I assume you sense the value and financial potential in network marketing. You know the power of our industry and what it can mean to you and others who build a successful business with you. Some of us, though, view the benefits of our business with *such* conviction that we inadvertently go too far in our assumptions. See if you can identify with any of the following ways we commonly lose perspective in the face of our passion:

"Everyone should do this!"

It is easy to become so excited about our industry that we act as if everyone should join us. Although having this much excitement is terrific, don't turn it into a firmly held belief! *Not* everyone is cut out to do this—nor do we need everyone to be. Have some fun and remind yourself why you *don't* want everyone on your team.

For instance, even though professionals are flocking to our industry, I want some to remain in their current jobs. We need individuals to remain as financial advisors to help us know where to invest our residual income; accountants to help us keep our taxes straight; and physicians to keep us healthy enough to fully enjoy our success.

There is a more substantial reason we don't need everyone to respond to our business: Wealth in this industry is not created when one person goes out and single-handedly recruits vast numbers of people; it is developed through the power of exponential growth. All that is necessary is for you to get a few people who in turn get a few more who keep repeating this process. As the awesome power of mathematical progression begins, so does a revenue stream of residual income that has no limits.

"People are dumb not to join us."

You may have heard the quip, "You don't need to be smart to do this business, but you have to be stupid not to do it!" It is a good one-liner, but don't adopt this as a real attitude. There are many legitimate reasons why people don't join us. Don't judge their "no." Just accept it. Prospects give us the freedom to honestly share our business with them, and in return, we need to give them the freedom to honestly respond to us.

"If someone says 'no' then I failed."

If someone declines to join you in your business it is not a referendum on you or your business. We are not in sales with the goal of "closing" everyone. Remember the following:

- We are in the business of sharing, not selling.
- We are in the business of presenting, not persuading.
- We are in the business of "show and tell." We show people our business and tell our story: why we are involved, why we are excited, how it works, and the types of individuals we are looking for.

"Showing my business to someone becomes a contest or competition."

Have you ever started a presentation with a goal to clearly explain the business, only to find that, somewhere along the way, your goal shifted to "winning" a verbal sparring match? I have done this. It is easy to get into subtle power struggles with people and forget our original purpose. When this happens, we end up shifting our strategy to *convincing* them that we are right to embrace network marketing and that they are wrong not to — we are wise and they are foolish. If you are inclined to do this, remind yourself during the presentation that:

- You want to engage this prospect in a *conversation*, not in a competition.
- You want to be in a *dialogue* with this person, not in a debate with them.
- Your goal is to *present* your business, not to have a power struggle.

- You don't want to talk this person into a "yes." If you have to push people into the business, you will probably have to pull them along after they get in.

How to Take a "No" in Stride

What is the best way to ensure that you take every "no" in stride? Adopt the following two vital mindsets in relation to your business:

Differentiate Responsibility, Task, and Desire

- Our *responsibility* is to consistently *expose* new people to our business.
- Our *task* is to *explain* our business with clarity, brevity, and honesty.
- Our *desire* is to find a *few* motivated individuals to repeat the process with us.

Once you get your business in front of a new person, you have already succeeded. Your success is not based on his or her response.

Differentiate Activity Goals and Results Goals

As easy as it is to confuse *activity* goals with *results* goals, it is important to remember that they are by no means the same, and this confusion only leads to discouragement. Activity goals are the numerical goals you set for yourself and those on your team—these include the number of times you want to present your business to new prospects. If your goal is to do this two times per week and you accomplish it, then you have met your goal—you have succeeded.

Results goals reflect the number of people you would like to see *responding* to your business each week or month. You cannot control these goals the way you can control your activity goals, so it's important to remember this distinction; when you separate the two, it becomes much easier to keep sharing your business with others consistently because you know that good results will eventually follow good activity.

Keep a Light Heart

Most of us enjoy being in the company of people like Mike and Barbara Lammons. They are upbeat, lighthearted, and confident enough to relax and be who they are. Learn to bring these qualities into your business presentation. You can be completely serious about your business and still maintain a fun attitude while sharing it with others. Be careful that your enthusiasm doesn't turn into overwhelming intensity. People will respond much more positively to you *and* your business if they sense that you are calm, confident, and enjoying just sharing your story with them.

How do you learn to be serious about your business and keep a light heart while sharing it with prospects? Developing a "fun mindset" will keep your business presentation enjoyable and will lift the pressure of worrying about the results of the meeting. One practical way of doing this is to imagine you are playing "Where's Waldo?"

Have you ever seen the children's picture book, *Where's Waldo?* When my girls were young, this was one of my favorite books to read and look at with them while we snuggled at bedtime. In the book, Waldo, the main character, is pictured in every illustration—for example, there is a drawing of a beach scene crowded with hundreds of people and it is the reader's task to spot Waldo in their midst. You find yourself eagerly scanning the picture trying to find the one person who is Waldo. There are many people sketched to look very similar to him at first glance, and just when you think you have found him, you usually realize it is someone who *looked* like him, but in fact was *not* the real Waldo.

This is all we are doing in our business — we are just playing "Where's Waldo." We scan the crowds of our daily world and look for who might be one of the special individuals we can work and dream with. So when someone tells you "no," remind yourself that it was a simple case of mistaken identity. In the privacy of your mind, you can have fun and say things like, "Oh! Excuse me. I thought you were Waldo but you are not." Or, in our case, you might say kiddingly to yourself:

Oh! Excuse me, I thought you might be an entrepreneur, but you are not.

Oh! Excuse me, I thought you might see the power of network marketing, but you don't.

Oh! Excuse me, I thought you might be up for joining me in my vision, but you are not.

Oh! Excuse me, I thought you might like to be a part of my team, but you don't.

Oh! Excuse me, I mistook you for someone I was looking for, but you are not that person. I'm sorry. Have a good day.

Learn to keep a light heart while being serious about your business! Enjoy the journey to success. You don't have to wait until you "arrive" before you can be joyful. Have fun and learn to laugh at those moments when you were sure you had found "Waldo" but it turned out to be somebody else.

A "Yes" is Good, but a "No" is Also Okay

As you share your business with others, don't be like the restaurant server who became over-identified with his work. Learn to enjoy those moments when someone says "yes" and also those when someone says "no." If you and those on your team are consistently exposing new people to your business, then a steadily increasing residual income is inevitable – no matter which people, or how many, say "no." Keep dreaming. Keep sharing your business with others, and keep a light heart. We are just looking for "Waldo."

CHAPTER
SEVEN

FEAR: MAKE IT YOUR FRIEND

Do you remember playing the game "hide-and-seek"? As a child I liked to play it with friends on warm summer nights and with my own kids when they were young as well. You know how it works: With eyes closed, one player counts in a loud voice to some designated number as all the other players run off to find places to hide. When the counter is finished, he calls out, "Ready or not, here I come!" and proceeds to seek out the other players.

When playing this game, most of us wanted a hiding spot so good that we would be extremely difficult to find—it was exciting to have thought of the perfect hiding place. But did you ever find a spot that was so good you couldn't be found at all? What did you begin to do after several minutes of not being discovered? You probably started to call out, make some noise, whistle, or throw something. Why? Because you had found a spot so good it was bor-

ing! You wanted to bring a little excitement back into the game.

I find that many adults are still playing hide-and-seek, especially in the area of career. They seek a place that is safe and secure and then hide there. Over time, some of these people discover that their hiding place is so excessively safe that it's boring. It offers no excitement, and there is little chance of being discovered, developed, fully utilized, challenged, or compensated. At some point, these people will decide if they want to remain safely hidden or make some noise, attract some attention, and get back into the game of life in which risk, fear, excitement, and success are all involved.

"Network marketing is the gathering place of individuals who don't want to spend their lives hiding."

Network marketing is the gathering place of individuals who don't want to spend their lives hiding. It attracts those who want to take some risks and taste success. The next time someone joins your team, take a moment to admire what is really happening. These people are doing more than becoming part of your downline and your company; they are making a statement of boldness and courage that deserves to be respected. New participants deserve to have our finest help and best assistance as they take their first steps on the journey that can wonderfully change their lives.

To help others (and ourselves) successfully complete this journey, it helps to understand the one thing all of us will encounter: fear. Fear is something we need to embrace, not avoid; we need to make fear our friend. To do this, it helps to understand the power of fear, how it works and, most importantly, how to minimize it so that fear is an appropriate presence rather than a dominant force in our lives. In this chapter, I will explain what fear is and how it influences all of us. In the next chapter, I will explain how people learn to successfully manage fear. (Please note that I am only attempting to address fear as it relates generally to your business. Trauma and acute fear are obviously beyond the scope of this writing.)

Understanding Fear

What is fear? Psychologically, fear is an emotional state. It is nature's warning system, alerting us to danger and triggering the well-known "fight-or-flight" response. Fear is an extremely important part of the survival instinct and its sole purpose is to protect us from harm.

In our lives, of course, fear can be a blessing and a curse—always well intentioned, but not always helpful. In some cases, it can literally save a life; in others, it can prevent people from living full lives. When fear plays too big a role, it can be as crippling as polio and as deadly as cancer. It can immobilize and overwhelm people. Misunderstanding fear has cost some entrepreneurs in network marketing their dreams and has prevented them from reaching their full potential.

It's important to understand that fear does not create itself nor does it occur in a vacuum. There are two things to keep in mind about fear:

Fear is Usually a Learned Response

There are few things that humans instinctively fear. Most of our fears are behavioral responses we learned from others through example or instruction—and whatever we learned can also be "unlearned." For example, as an executive coach, I help adults let go of fears that are irrational, unhealthy, counterproductive, or just plain silly. This is "unlearning." But, as a parent, I spend time teaching my fearless adolescent daughters that there are some things in life that we really *should* fear.

What have you learned from others about fear? Did the influential people in your life model boldness, confidence, a "can do" attitude, or some other positive disposition? Or did they model an attitude that left you worried about your ability to cope in the world? While it is important to be aware of what you picked up from others, it is far more important to know that you can transcend these things. You are not stuck.

An Underlying Thought or Belief Always Accompanies Fear

The emotion of fear is always connected to an underlying thought, perception, or belief—which, be aware, need not be accurate. It simply needs to be present and unchallenged to have an impact. This means fear often gets triggered by observations and incorrect interpretations. The result? A "false alarm." Do you recall being a young child and thinking there was a scary creature under your bed? That was a false alarm. It's the same thing when a fire alarm goes off and there is no real fire. Once the *perception* of fire occurs, everything else goes into motion: alarms sound, people evacuate, fire trucks arrive, all because of a false alarm.

When we experience a false fear alarm, it sets a number of physiological responses in motion: adrenalin is released, our cardiovascular system is activated, and our musculature prepares for "fight or flight." It is exhausting for people to live with false alarms. It steals their joy, erodes their energy, and ages them prematurely. In network marketing, false alarms cause some people to run and hide, fleeing their dreams, abandoning their hopes, and losing financial freedom. We'll look at this effect in more detail shortly as we consider the ways fear impacts our lives.

The Impact of Fear

Many a college student, while pursuing "knowledge of the self," briefly entertain the idea of becoming psychologists; while most quickly abandon the desire (they discover most of the material to be boring and the people weird!), the brief foray into the field exposes them to a very powerful concept: *approach-avoidance.* This concept is extremely useful in understanding how fear impacts our decisions and behavior—sometimes without our even realizing it—and has immediate relevance in the entrepreneurial world of network marketing. In its simplest form, approach-avoidance is just what it sounds like. It is the desire to simultaneously approach and avoid something. It is feeling pushed in one direction and pulled in another. We express this frame of mind when we say that we are torn, betwixt and between, between a rock and a hard place, or unable to make up our mind. Approach-avoidance is like driving your car and wanting to put the gearshift in both drive and reverse at the same time.

This pattern occurs every day in network marketing. Have you ever felt torn about making a phone call? Or contacting a prospect who intimidates you but could be huge in your business? How about following up with people to learn whether or not they have decided to join your team? That feeling of ambivalence is the presence of approach-avoidance.

In real life, this simple concept has profound consequences. Let me give you an example and then show how it relates to our pursuit of dreams in network marketing:

Joe: Joe is a good friend of mine. Several years ago, I was watching him go back and forth in his relationship with his girlfriend. He could not decide if he should marry her. At one point, he could not imagine living without her and would pursue the relationship with full force. Then, as he got closer to the actual commitment of marriage, he would suddenly lose interest, have doubts, and back away.

For me as an observer, it was like watching Joe drive a car. When marriage was far off in the distance, it looked extremely attractive to Joe. Figuratively speaking, he would jump into his car, put it in drive, and step on the accelerator. He could not get to marriage fast enough. He would be driving forward at 40, 50, 60, and 70 miles per hour. But as he got closer and closer to commitment, Joe began to feel increasingly fearful — he would take his foot off of the accelerator, reach for the brake, and slow down. Finally, he would come to a dead stop, put the car in reverse, and back

> out of his commitment. After he had retreated so far that marriage was no longer on the horizon, Joe's fear would subside; feeling better, he would decide that he actually *did* want to marry this woman and start the entire cycle all over again.

Without knowing it, Joe was caught in approach-avoidance. His behavior was a function of two differing emotions within him: desire and fear. Look at the graph below:

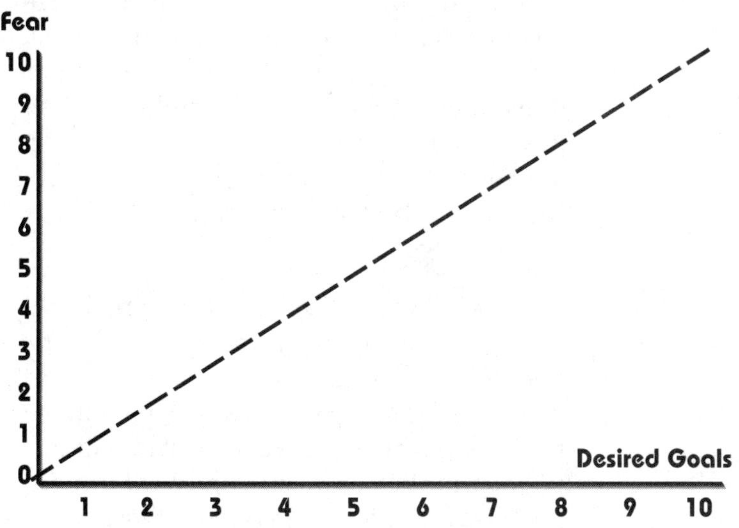

Notice that fear moves in tandem with the pursuit of a goal. As we approach the desired goal, the level of fear increases. As we avoid the desired goal, the fear decreases.

This pattern is identical to what happens to many people in network marketing. Let's look at Brad and his network marketing business:

Brad: Brad loved the thought of being financially free one day in the future. He had always dreamed of being his own boss, having free time, ample finances, and no need to report to an employer every day. Understanding that network marketing was the perfect vehicle to help him achieve this, Brad jumped in, ready to drive his business toward his dreams. Like Joe, he got into the car, put it in drive, and stomped on the accelerator. He couldn't go fast enough when he grasped the power of exponential growth and residual income. He filled out his application, went to trainings, and bought materials to get started properly. With the windows rolled down and the radio cranked up, Brad started to zoom toward his goal while singing at the top of his lungs. Life never looked so good.

Further down the road, though, it occurred to Brad that to be successful, he needed to actually do some things that were uncomfortable to him. He realized he was going to have to contact some people, make some calls, and talk about his business. He would have to work hard, be persistent, and encounter many people who were clueless about the joy of being a successful entrepreneur in network marketing. As Brad began to acknowledge these realities, he did as Joe had done, he took his foot off the accelerator, slowed down, and backed up. When the discomfort subsided, he once again began to attend meetings, read books, and get ready

> to drive his business forward. Eventually, Brad became one of those who "hang around." He never quit, but he never did much. He was lost in the nether world of those who wanted to hang on to their dreams while not doing anything that created anxiety.

Sound familiar? Why does this happen in network marketing? How can a person dream about being very bold but then not take action? How can a person intend to make an important call, set up a critical meeting, or broach the subject of business with a friend, and then suddenly wimp out? Why do people avoid doing the very things they want to do and know are necessary for their success? Because the *desire to avoid fear can obscure every other dream and goal*.

Have you ever been driving down a busy highway at high speeds and watched someone suddenly cross over several lanes of traffic to make an abrupt exit? Practically speaking, this is what fear does to people — it causes them to make abrupt exits from the pursuit of their dreams and goals.

People make these abrupt exits because they do not know how to manage fear, anxiety, and discomfort. When they begin to experience a certain level of discomfort, a *literal shift occurs* in their goals and desires. Their goal is no longer to build a successful network marketing business, attain wealth, or prepare for their financial future; their new goal, and for the moment their *only* goal, is to get rid of the discomfort. They want the fear to be gone! Until this occurs, they have no other priorities, passions, or pursuits. Relief is their only objective. This is the power of fear when we do not properly understand and manage it—which brings us back to how "false alarms" affect your business.

How Faulty Beliefs Trigger False Alarms

Have you ever attempted to phone someone you have not spoken with for quite a while and heard the automated message that says, "The number you are trying to reach is not in service," or, "That number has been changed. The new number is . . . "?

This happens whenever we attempt to contact someone based on old information that is no longer current. The phone number was correct in the past, but it is no longer accurate. Most people simply update their databases with the person's new phone number to be current again, no big deal.

> ***"The desire to avoid fear can obscure every other dream and goal."***

We need to do the same thing with our minds when it comes to fear. In the same way that many of us update our address books along with our computers, software, and files, we need to update the memory banks and databases of our minds. Our minds need to be upgraded and cleaned out periodically. Unfortunately, few of us were ever taught to do this, and many adults go through life on information that is very old, no longer accurate, and possibly may never have been accurate in the first place.

This was the problem with my friend Joe who was fearful of marriage. After watching him go through several cycles of approach-avoidance, I asked him to join me for a cup of coffee. I was curious if there was old information urging him to run from the altar.

Initially, Joe had no *idea* why he did what he did, he just knew he backed away whenever he became uncomfortable. His goal was to simply get rid of his fear and discomfort. He never attempted to *understand* the fear. He did not know where he had learned it or to what beliefs it was connected. To Joe, it was an emotion that would appear out of nowhere and then vanish when he put the relationship in reverse.

As we talked, Joe and I stopped looking at the "bobber on the surface of the water" to learn what was happening at the "hook level." Joe told me his story: As a young boy, Joe thought he was part of a secure and happy family, but when Joe was five years old, his parents told him they were getting a divorce. On that day, the safety of Joe's little five-year-old world blew up, and his five-year-old brain put some very important information in his database. This information said that marriage is scary because, like gunpowder, it can blow up in your face at any time. It became a core belief of his that marriage was unsafe, unwise, and to be avoided no matter how much you thought you loved someone. For many years, this belief lay dormant in Joe, and only showed up when he fell in love. It tried to give Joe good advice that was only meant to protect him from harm, but the advice was old and no longer accurate. (This is why I say that fear always means well but it is not always helpful.)

As Joe and I chatted, he began to embrace his fear and admit that he was perfectly entitled to be afraid when he was five years old. He also gave himself permission to admit that he no longer needed to view marriage from the very limited vantage point of a five-year-old boy. He gave himself permission to acknowledge that he did not have to replicate his parents' mistakes. Most importantly,

Joe allowed himself to upgrade, update, and change his database concerning marriage. When he "unlearned" some old beliefs and installed some new ones, he was free to push through his discomfort. Today, Joe has what can only be described as a world-class marriage and family.

What about You?

Could it be time for some mental spring-cleaning in your life? When was the last time you looked at the files you have been collecting about yourself over the years? Many people are surprised to discover that they are limiting their ability to believe in their own success based on old experiences or perceptions that have had too much control over their lives for far too long. These old beliefs keep causing false alarms that are truly costly.

Fear Comes in Different Sizes

It helps to remember that fear is simply an emotion with varying levels of intensity. The diagram below illustrates the range of various degrees of fear:

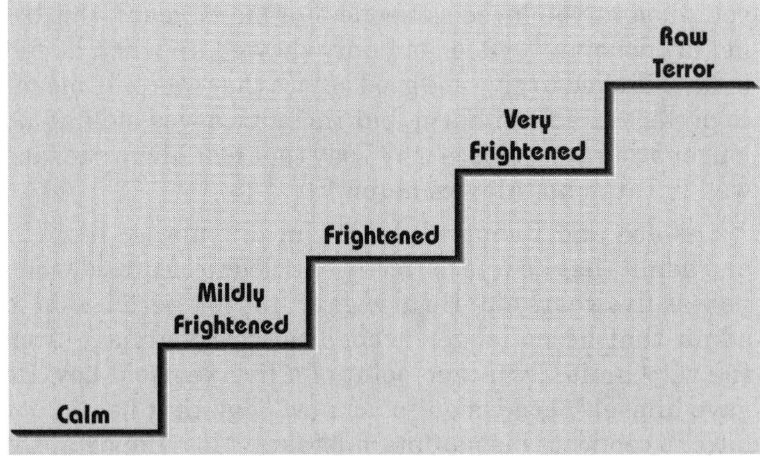

A mistake some people make is attempting to orchestrate their lives to be devoid of *any* level of discomfort. The moment they experience even a modest amount of anxiety or fear, they begin to pull away from the cause. When this becomes a behavioral pattern, they exit every opportunity for growth and success when their arbitrary threshold of discomfort is reached. This is a very expensive coping strategy.

Hide-and-seek is a great game for kids, but as adults, we need to be sure that fear has not kept us in hiding for too long. Maybe it is time for you to look at the "seek" side of life. Maybe it is time to stand up and make some noise, to be found and discovered as a person with vision, talent, and drive. Maybe it is time to drive your business, reach your goals, and discover financial freedom. To do so, all you need to do is learn to effectively manage your fear. We will learn how in the next chapter.

CHAPTER
EIGHT

FEAR: MANAGE IT LIKE A PRO

Have you ever watched *The Wizard of Oz*? It is a movie that deserves to be an enduring classic. Do you remember what happened at the end of the movie when Dorothy and her friends finally got to meet the Wizard? At first, they were filled with fear as they interacted with the Wizard's booming, disembodied voice. When, with trepidation, they risked disagreeing with the Wizard, he reacted with an even louder and more threatening voice. He was indignant that anyone would challenge "the great and mighty Wizard of Oz." Just as Dorothy and her friends were feeling overwhelmed by the force of this voice, Toto, Dorothy's dog, ran to the source of the sound and pulled back a curtain to reveal a small, sweet man not nearly as frightening as they had perceived.

Fear is much like the Wizard of Oz. Left unchallenged, it can seem incredibly powerful, but when we pull the

curtains back and see fear for what it is, we find it to be not nearly the imposing force we imagined. We no longer need to avoid or run from it.

True entrepreneurs understand that courage is not the *absence* of fear. Indeed, fear is the quiet chronic companion of *all* entrepreneurs in the early stages of pursuing their dreams. Courage is the ability to move forward in the *presence* of fear. Successful entrepreneurs are well acquainted with fear, anxiety, and doubt—they have just learned to give fear less authority and less influence in their lives.

"Courage is the ability to move forward in the presence of fear."

This week, I was asked to have lunch with Paul. He is 38 years old, married, and has three young children. Paul just accepted a job as president and C.E.O. of a new Internet company. Currently, the company consists only of a few employees, one technological idea that has yet to be developed, and some seed money. All that's left to do is find the right management, technical, and investment people, create and test the product, fine-tune and market it, get the company profitable, court venture capitalists, raise multiple millions of dollars, prepare for an initial public offering, survive the IPO, and then continue to sustain and manage the growth while finding new expansion opportunities to keep the stock valuation strong—your run-of-the-mill monumental endeavor. Nothing to it.

Before taking on this task, Paul was the president of a well-established, smooth-running corporation and just two months away from being fully vested in it. He left it all, including a salary well over four hundred thousand dollars per year—to earn a fraction of that while growing this company. Do you think Paul doesn't know fear as his constant companion? Bank on it—he does. He just won't give it undue authority or influence in his life.

We need to do the same thing. There are skills and attitudes we can emulate that are common to all entrepreneurs who have learned to successfully manage fear. When you learn to keep these in mind, you'll find the pursuit and enjoyment of your success to be much easier. You can learn to quiet the voice of fear, make it your friend, and then get on with pursuing your dream.

Secret #1: Learn to Welcome Fear

Learn to be grateful for the presence of fear. Fear can be indicative of some wonderful things in our lives. It is often the indicator that we have a rich, active relationship to life; it lets us know we are alive! It is the evidence that we are growing, stretching, and pushing the limits of our abilities. Responding correctly to fear has a way of developing our competence, character, and skills. Welcoming fear is what allows us to expand the borders of our daily world—and embracing fear is the precursor to success in network marketing.

Some people spend inordinate amounts of time trying to keep fear out of their lives all together. It is as if they are attempting to build a wall around their lives that will keep fear and discomfort at a safe distance. They try to keep their lives organized, structured, and secure, and begin to do only those things that are within the perimeter of their known world. If something doesn't look safe, familiar, and easy to do, they will avoid it. People who arrange their lives around the desire for security are often shocked in the end when the walls they built for self-protection turn out to be their own self-constructed prison. It didn't keep fear out of their lives; it kept them out of living.

Learn to face your fear. Find out what makes you anxious about the pursuit of your dream and the growth of your business. Remember that all successful people are intimately acquainted with fear. They know what it is to be scared but not stopped; to be frightened but not frozen; to be uncomfortable but undaunted. If you want to join them in success, you will also need to join them in welcoming fear as a natural part of life.

Secret #2: Remember That You Are Surrounded by Courage

In moments of fear, doubt, or anxiety, it is easy to become so focused on our own discomfort, we forget to notice that we are surrounded by demonstrations of quiet courage. Following are a few that I admire:

- At the beginning of every school year, we are surrounded by quiet courage. Notice the kindergarten children who get on the bus for the first time. They wonder how they will find the right bus at the end of the day and how they will know where to get off. Note the freshmen boys who go into high school and wonder if it is true that the upper classmen will make them push a penny down the hall with their noses. Pay attention to the college freshmen who kiss their parents goodbye and venture out on their own for the first time. All of them are models of quiet courage in the midst of quiet fear.

- How about college graduates who go out for that first interview? How about homemakers who apply for a job after being out of the workforce for years? How about those who have just lost a job because of downsizing, mergers, etc., only to pick up and start looking for a new one? How about those who have been looking for a job, have been turned down dozens of times, but have continued to apply? Quiet courage.
- How about those who don't know the power of network marketing and consequently go every day to a job they dread? Their bosses are abusive, their work uninspiring, but they keep showing up because they are committed to providing for their families the best way they know. Quiet courage.
- How about those who remain in marginal marriages because they want their children to avoid the trauma of divorce? Noble love. Quiet courage.
- How about those in abusive marriages who finally decide to get out? Quiet courage.
- How about the thousands of people in network marketing who every day make one more call, initiate one more meeting, and encourage one more person in their downline even when they feel weary? Unsung heroes. Quiet courage.

The next time you are aware of experiencing discomfort in the pursuit of your dream, look around. Every day, people who exhibit acts of noble character, great love, and quiet courage surround you. Join them.

Secret #3: Pursue Excellence, Not Perfection

Some people get bogged down in the growth of their business because they have confused excellence with perfection. Be aware that there is a significant difference between the two—the pursuit of excellence is a goal; the pursuit of perfection is a curse.

A surprising number of people have adopted the belief that they *must* do things perfectly. It is a fatal attempt to approach life on the pass/fail grading method. (This is an academic grading method in which the only grades given are pass or fail—there is no "A, B, C, D, or F.")

"The pursuit of excellence is a goal. The pursuit of perfection is a curse."

This approach to life is usually learned at an early age, installed by an authority figure with a special knack for telling people what they did wrong instead of what they did well. For example, imagine a young child who is learning to clean up the kitchen. After dinner, this child attempts to clean the entire kitchen to the best of his ability. When he finishes, he is proud and eager for his parents to come in and review the work. What happens if, instead of praising the child for the ten things done well, the parents shame or scold him for not folding a towel correctly? If this happens repeatedly, the child learns not to pursue excellence and enjoy the satisfaction that accompanies it, but instead to pursue perfection in order to avoid feeling like a failure.

Perfectionists who see the world as a pass/fail grading system generally wind up failing in their own minds. Talk to them sometime after they have just done something very well; they will tell you that it was "not as good as it appeared to be," or that they "just got lucky." In either case, they are not free to savor their own success. Additionally, the desire to do things perfectly slows them down because they spend too much time worrying, planning, and fearing some mishap before they take their first simple steps as an entrepreneur.

If you or someone on your team is caught in the trap of perfectionism, pay close attention to the next secret.

Secret #4: Give Yourself Permission to Learn and Make Mistakes

Have you ever watched people play golf on television? I used to detest golf. The game looked ridiculously simple and boring to me. How difficult could it be to stand up and whack a golf ball with a club? Then I tried to play the game and discovered that there was far more to it than met the eye. Network marketing is like this. It appears to be so easy. All you do is get in, find a few others who will join you, keep repeating the process, and live happily ever after, right?

Wrong! Like golf, network marketing is both ingeniously simple and, at times, maddeningly difficult. There is far more to it than is immediately obvious, and it requires a significant learning curve. You need to give yourself permission to make mistakes and have spectacular failures on your path to success.

Learning how to listen to prospects, knowing when to bring up your business, and knowing how to relate it to a prospect's life situation is a skill. Learning to shut up and stop "George Bushing" all over your prospects is a skill. Learning how to help those on your team—including yourself—stay focused and motivated is a skill. Learning how to think and work as an entrepreneur is a skill. Learning how to lead people over whom you have no formal authority is a skill. Learning how to dream and teach others to do the same is a skill. These skills take time to develop, and it can be a relief to become aware of this fact. Give yourself the freedom to cultivate the skills you need to succeed.

It's been said, "Before a company can be great, it's got to be good. Before a company can be good, it's got to be bad. And before a company can be bad, it's got to get started." This is also true of you and me in the pursuit of our dreams. We cannot be great before we are good. We cannot be good before we are bad. And we cannot even do our business badly until we get started!

Don't think that you can or need to be great in the early stages of your business. As Les Brown says, "You don't have to be great before you can get started, but you have to get started before you can be great." Be patient with yourself and others as you learn the skills necessary for success. All entrepreneurs have tasted failure, big and small, before they have tasted success. Don't fear making your mistakes—accept them. Keep a light heart, keep learning, and keep working. As one Fortune 500 corporation reminds its employees, "Fail often. But fall forward."

Secret #5: Throw Away Your Electron Microscope!

Have you ever seen a picture of dust-mites? They are prehistoric-looking microbes that must be the ugliest creatures on the planet—no chance of ever winning the "most lovable pet" contest. Advertisers usually show them in pictures, after being magnified over ten thousand times their actual size, and then they remind us that these ugly things live in our beds! Why do advertisers do this? Because they know the actual size of these creatures would not evoke any reaction in us. But when we see one blown up to look as big as a triceratops and imagine it crawling around in our bed, it makes us either want to buy whatever they are selling or learn to sleep like a horse... standing up.

This is what some people do in their own minds. They take everything that causes them anxiety and put them under an electron microscope. Then they magnify the image ten thousand times over and scare themselves to death in the process! If you tend to blow unpleasant moments out of proportion, then learn to stop putting them under the microscope.

Look at any computer with a "zoom" control in the tool bar to learn how the mind can work for us or against us. On my computer, zoom control allows me to adjust how I view something on the screen. I have the option of enlarging an image up to 500 percent or reducing it to ten percent of its original size. Notice the difference between seeing the word "fear" enlarged...

FEAR

...and seeing its size dramatically reduced...

FEAR

If you like, type the words "I am competent" on your computer and play with the zoom control. Blow the words up to 500 percent, then reduce them to ten percent, and be aware of how dramatic or insignificant the impact can be depending simply on which computer keys you press.

Some people, particularly those who live with excessive worry or fear, habitually play with the zoom control of their minds. If a thought is negative or unpleasant, they will zoom in on it and magnify it far out of proportion. Others will take a thought that is positive, pleasant, or hopeful, and reduce it to only ten percent of its original size. Over time, the printout of their lives reflects what has been most prominently displayed on the computer screen of the mind.

In the growth of your business, which of the following thoughts do you minimize and maximize? Which ones do you zoom in on and which ones do you reduce?

WHAT DO YOU FOCUS ON?

My discomfort .... My dream

My anxiety .... My ambition

My hassles........... My hopes

My frustrations ...... My faith

My fatigue........... My fun

My struggles......... My success

Many things in life are like dust-mites—if you blow them out of proportion, they will give you the creeps, but if you keep them in perspective, you may not like them, but you can still sleep like a baby.

Secret #6: You Only Ski Five Feet at a Time

I recently returned from a week of skiing in Switzerland. The panoramic view from the Matterhorn at 12,000 feet is sublime beyond description. The first morning I was at the top of the mountain trying to memorize the view before skiing the five miles down into Italy for lunch at a mountainside restaurant. Just prior to pushing off, I glanced over at one of my friends. His expression suggested that the view had taken his breath away . . . not because of its beauty, but because he was trying to figure out how he was going to ski all the way to our destination. To him, the slopes looked too steep, too long, and too difficult. He was definitely feeling overwhelmed at what lay before him.

This is how many people feel when beginning a network marketing business. They wonder, "How will I ever complete the journey? How will I ever become a top income earner? How will I ever attain the higher leadership positions? How will I ever become as confident, poised, and knowledgeable as so-and-so at the meeting?"

May I suggest to you the same thing I did to my friend? In his moments of anxiety, I encouraged him to stop looking at the *entire* mountain. There was no need for him to attempt to absorb the full scope of what he had to do. Because his skis were five feet long, he could only ski *five feet at a time*. All he needed to do was look at the terrain immediately in front of him. Later, as we ate our lunch outside in the sun, he looked up and was astonished by the fear he had conquered and how far he had come. By the end of the week, he was flying down the mountain with great pride, full confidence, and without fear. Why? Because he had learned to ski five feet at a time.

In those moments when you feel anxious or overwhelmed, remember to simplify your task. All you need to do is what is right in front of you. Complete that and focus on the next task that lies before you. Start skiing five feet at a time. Do this long enough, and one day *you* will be a top income earner and leader who others look to and hope to emulate.

Secret #7: Remember What is Truly Frightening

There are certain realities successful entrepreneurs have learned to accept. They know:

- *You cannot know the exhilaration of winning without also knowing the sensations of fear or failure.*
- *You cannot enjoy future financial freedom if you insist on avoiding fear in the present.*
- *You cannot grow a large profitable network marketing business without growing as a person.*

But entrepreneurs are not fearless. Do you want to know what makes entrepreneurs afraid?

- *Having dreams that never become realities.*
- *Having talent that is not utilized.*
- *Having potential that goes undeveloped.*

- *Giving the best of themselves to employers, instead of being self-employed.*
- *Wishing for more money but never having it.*
- *Desiring to create memories with those they love but not having enough time or money to do so.*
- *Desiring to be a blessing to others but not having the time or money to do so.*
- *Giving the best years of their lives and the best hours of their days to a boss's dreams instead of their own.*
- *Learning too late that success is far more easily achieved than they believed.*

To entrepreneurs, the above list is *far* more disconcerting than the intermittent fear that is part of pursuing success. What entrepreneurs fear is a life lived in the narrow confines of one's comfort zone. They know that avoiding fear is equivalent to avoiding life. They know "playing it safe" is not a life at all, but a slow death.

Network marketing is far more than an invitation to create financial freedom—it is an invitation to take an active part in your life. Entrepreneurs RSVP saying they will be there, no matter what.

CHAPTER
NINE

GOLF COURSE ECONOMICS

The finest lesson in economics I ever received lasted less than 30 seconds. It did not occur while pursuing one of my two masters degrees or in my doctoral studies, nor did it come from a book or seminar, or from my experience in the corporate world. It happened in graduate school as I played a round of golf with some friends.

All of us were young, all of us were broke, and we were playing on a golf course surrounded by million-dollar homes. After looking at one spectacular home after another, I finally exclaimed, "What in the world do these people do to be able to afford these homes?" Without hesitation one of my friends responded, "It's easy, Tom. The people living in those homes either have money working for them or they have people working for them."

"Money working for them or people working for them...." The impact of these words never left me. After

hearing them, my challenge was to find a way to have them become true for me. I wanted to find a way to experience what he was talking about and to be able to afford the type of home that had led to my original question.

While pondering his comment year after year, I did what most people do—I got busy with life and making a living. And even though I was able to make a very *good* living, I knew I was not living as an entrepreneur. I had to keep working to keep my revenue stream flowing. I discovered that making good money without having the time to enjoy it was not particularly rewarding. It became obvious that quality of life is a function of simultaneously having time and money. I did not want to wait until I was 65 years old to have money and time together—I have seen too many people lose their health just when they finally had money and time.

Eventually, it occurred to me that even though I was in the top one percent of income earners, I was nothing more than an hourly worker. I was living by linear income. I had to keep working to keep getting paid. My revenue stream was like a garden hose. If I kept working, the money would flow through the hose like water. But, when I stopped, it was like taking a garden hose and bending it so that the flow of water was blocked. For instance, because I was paid by billable hours, when I took time off to travel or vacation with my family, I would always calculate the money I lost by not working and then add in the cost of the activity.

When I looked at my friends' lives, I realized they were caught in the same web. It did not matter if they were physicians, lawyers, dentists, or accountants. They *all* had to keep working to keep getting paid. Nor did it matter if they were paid $10, $100, or $1000 per hour. It was the same obligation. It was still linear income—hours exchanged for dollars—and not even *close* to financial freedom.

Years later, when I grasped the wisdom of network marketing, I realized that it was the perfect way to "have people work for you and have money work for you." At the end of this chapter, I will explain how and why network marketing is a unique mechanism for financial freedom. But first, let's look at some financial realities and then explore what most of us have been taught about money, work, and being an entrepreneur. It will help you understand why I was, as thousands of others are, slow to comprehend the financial potential in building a successful network marketing business.

Smelling Salts for Financial Reality

Most dentists have smelling salt on hand in case a patient faints. It helps to clear the senses and snap people back to consciousness. Following are some "financial smelling salts" that can clear our senses and snap us back into reality:

> **Reality #1:** Most people have been taught how to work for money. They have not been taught how money works.

> **Reality #2:** Most people make just enough money to qualify to get into debt. They do not make enough money to get out of debt or avoid it completely.

> **Reality #3:** You are not "well off" until you can take time off and still live well.

> **Reality #4:** Being around money is not the same thing as having money.

Reality #5: Most people prepare for retirement with a little bit of planning, a fair amount of hope, and a great deal of denial.

Reality #6: Income-producing assets are the key to financial freedom.

If you want to have an interesting discussion with friends, ask them what their parents taught them about money and finances. Stop and think about what your parents taught you. You will discover that many of us were taught some combination of the following:

- How to open a checking and savings account
- How to balance a checkbook
- How to get a credit card
- To avoid debt
- To pay our bills promptly
- To save for a home
- To find a "good job" with good benefits

Look at the above list and notice what it does *not* include—the most basic fact that there are only five things you can do with money (pay taxes, pay debt, spend it, invest it, or give it away.) There is no instruction about how money works and how wealth is created. There is little emphasis on the value of having time work for you and not against you in wealth creation. There is nothing said about the power of income-producing assets or how to create financial freedom at different income levels and ages. There is little mention of the joy of giving, and there is almost no encouragement to think and live as an entrepreneur.

Of course, parents' silence on these subjects does not reflect deficient love or concern. How can they teach their children what they don't know themselves? They are still scrambling to make ends meet and figure out how to get ready for their own retirement. They are still unaware of the simplicity of financial success—especially via network marketing.

Why Such Low Expectations of Financial Success?

When it comes to financial freedom, have you ever wondered why most people believe that it is impossible, or highly improbable, that they will ever live well and build wealth? Why do they accept that being an employee and not creating wealth is the norm and anything else is the exception? Why do they wish for more but do little about it? Why do they live most of their lives "hand-to-mouth?"

> ***"They either have money working for them or people working for them."***

Most people live this way because it is what they have been taught and had reinforced by families, friends, educators, and cultural norms. They have been trained and schooled to be good employees, to believe that working for someone else is the norm, and that anything else is the exception. They have been groomed for mediocrity and are rarely encouraged to take entrepreneurial risks.

Consider the following list of common expressions and note how all of them instill a belief or reminder that risk-taking (anything divergent from the norm) should be avoided. I would guess that you have heard most of these in the course of your life. By looking at the first half of each expression, you'll immediately know what follows. We are taught:

To play it . . . . safe.
Don't bite . . . . the hand that feeds you.
Don't rock . . . . the boat.
Don't make . . . . waves.
Don't take . . . . risks.
Don't take . . . . chances.
A bird in the hand . . . . . . is worth two in the bush.
There is a sucker . . . . born every minute.
If something sounds too good to be true . . . . . . it is.

There is an element of truth in each of the above expressions and times when they merit consideration. The problem is that the net effect of these common truisms is that they encourage people to stay where they are, accept the status quo, and not risk change, new ways of thinking, and new ways of succeeding.

Our educational systems further encourage and prepare us to be "employees." There are almost no courses offered on entrepreneurship, strategies for financial success, how to retire while young, and why financial freedom is easy. Look at what colleges and universities usually teach as preparation for entry into the work force:

WE ARE TAUGHT HOW TO...

- Research a company.
- Prepare a résumé.
- Get a "good job."
- Discover what our salary should be.
- Think of "salary" and "hourly wages."
- Interview effectively.
- Be "marketable."

WE ARE TRAINED TO...

- Have good job skills.
- Be employable.
- Work for someone else.
- Give the lion's share of our time and talent to further someone else's dreams.
- Give the best hours of the day and the best years of our lives to a job or career.
- Expect to work until we are 65.
- Be great workers, not to have great wealth.
- Be *employees,* not *entrepreneurs*.

Against this backdrop, it is easy to see why many people find it difficult to grasp the simplicity of achieving financial freedom and the quality of life available to an entrepreneur. They have been trained to live in bureaucratic time instead of entrepreneurial time. (For a review of these important concepts, see chapter four, "Living in Entrepreneurial Time," in *Dare to Dream and Work to Win.*) Individuals accept as an unquestionable tenet and irrevocable truth that most people should work because of necessity, not desire, until they are 65. They accept that getting a few weeks of vacation is a norm not to be challenged. They accept a lifetime subscription to daily commuting and fighting traffic.

Additionally, it is assumed that they will spend most of their lives as employees in a "one-down position" with little power and the employer holding all of the cards. They understand what Tennessee Ernie Ford meant when he sang, "Saint Peter don't you call me 'cause I can't go…I owe my soul to the company store." They accept always having to ask for things of the employer as favors. They assume it is perfectly normal to:

- Ask for an interview
- Ask for a job
- Ask permission to arrive late
- Ask permission to leave early
- Ask for a day off
- Ask for a vacation
- Ask for a promotion
- Ask for a pay raise

Anything different is foreign to their thinking and not part of their belief system. Consequently, even when they attempt to reach out and embrace the notion of financial success and freedom of time, their old beliefs act like quicksand and suck them back into the warm familiarity of a life going nowhere.

I Hope You Become Unemployable

I live in northern Virginia and this past winter we had one of those extraordinary February days when the temperature zooms up to 70 degrees. It was a spectacular day so I decided to go golfing. I called a friend who loves to golf and invited him to be my guest at my golf club. He was sorry I called. He was torn between the desire to golf and the inability to "drop everything" and join me. As we talked on the phone, he finally had to say, "I would love to golf today, Tom, but I cannot leave work."

He was implying that he did not have the authority, freedom, or prerogative to do what he wanted to on this exceptional day. I laughed and told him, "That's the problem with you. You are so good, so important, and so vital to that organization that you are not even free to leave unexpectedly for a day! I wish you could be unemployable like me. I am so unimportant that nobody cares if I work or play today! No one will decide for me how to spend my time. And no one will be upset that I am out there lovin' life on this beautiful day while you remain at your desk. It must be nice to be so vital to an organization that you are not free to leave and do what you want to." He laughed along with me and then said... something not suitable for print.

Strategies for Living Well and Creating Wealth

The unexpected popularity of the television show *Who Wants to be a Millionaire* has made it obvious that practically everyone would like to be a millionaire. The difficulty is that most people have a desire and that is all. They have no strategy, no plan, no timetable, or knowledge of how to do this. This leaves them wishing instead of working purposefully towards this very attainable goal. To achieve this goal, all we need to do is understand some very basic concepts and act on the advice I received years ago on the golf course.

Concept #1: Make the commitment to learn how money works instead of only thinking of new ways to work for money.

Concept #2: Learn to understand the role and value of time in the creation of wealth. Time is the universal commodity we all have, and when it comes to economic freedom, time is our best friend. Unfortunately, when it comes to financial planning and freedom, many people late in life look like an NFL team that is down by two touchdowns with two minutes remaining in the game. The clock is working against them, not for them, and they are forced into a "hurry up offense," hoping for the successful completion of a "Hail Mary" pass in the end zone. Start now learning how to get time on your side; thankfully, network marketing can provide a workable "hurry up offense" if needed.

Concept #3: Understand "the rule of 72." This well-known rule-of-thumb is a simple way to determine how long it will take your savings or investments to double in value. All you need to do is divide the number 72 by the rate at which your money is growing.

Example: If your money is growing at a rate of 15% then: 72 ÷ 15 = 4.8 years to double your money.

Example: If your money is growing at a rate of 20% then: 72 ÷ 20 = 3.6 years to double your money.

Currently, it is not uncommon for people to see a very strong rate of growth with their money, which means it is a very profitable era to earn money and invest it to work for you.

When the Lights Go On

When people begin to grasp how to make money work for them instead of just working for money, life looks completely different. They are suddenly infused with knowledge and hope. In turn, they begin to look for realistic strategies for producing revenue that can be invested and begin to grow as a function of time and interest. The genius of network marketing becomes doubly apparent at this point. It is a cost-effective and brilliant strategy for enabling people to enjoy both sources of "golf course economics" ...people and money working for them.

Noting the two income streams—stream one with *people* working for you, stream two with *money* working for you—there are logically only four options with these scenarios:

1. You have both people and money working for you.
2. You have people working for you but not money.
3. You have money working for you but not people.
4. You have neither money nor people working for you.

You know where most people are on this list.

Golf Course Economics

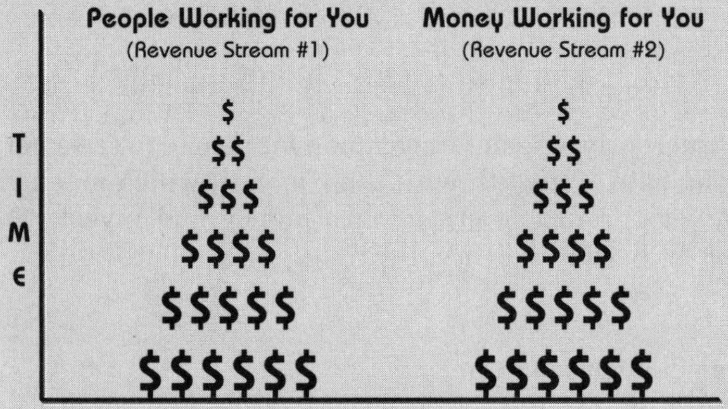

	People Working for You (Revenue Stream #1)	Money Working for You (Revenue Stream #2)
T	$	$
I	$$	$$
M	$$$	$$$
E	$$$$	$$$$
	$$$$$	$$$$$
	$$$$$$	$$$$$$

There are two income streams represented here that can create financial freedom: One is to have money working for you so that it earns more in the form of interest or dividends; the other is to be able to receive revenue from the productivity and success of others. In either case, you can have revenue coming to you without having to be present to earn it. Note that both of these increase substantially with time. Both are income-producing assets.

Get In on the Action

In today's economy, unprecedented numbers of people are beginning to see the power of having money work for them instead of just working for money. They are commonly seeing their investments double in size in a handful of years. Never has there been a better time to understand how this works and the role network marketing plays in making this possible.

If you are like many people, you might feel as if everyone around you is making a fortune in the stock market and becoming "instant millionaires" through a mutual fund or buying stock in a start-up company. Rather than lament the wealth being created by others, I suggest you develop a game plan of your own. There is no need to passively observe others begin to enjoy economic freedom when you can have it too.

How do you get invited into this party? How do you get in on the action? If you want to have money working for you, the old saying, "it takes money to make money" is true. The question is, how do you get started? How do you begin to carve out a riverbed that ultimately becomes a revenue stream producing a torrent of cash flow?

First, build stream #1 (people working for you). Let *this* become the source of revenue that begins to fill stream #2 (money working for you). It looks like this:

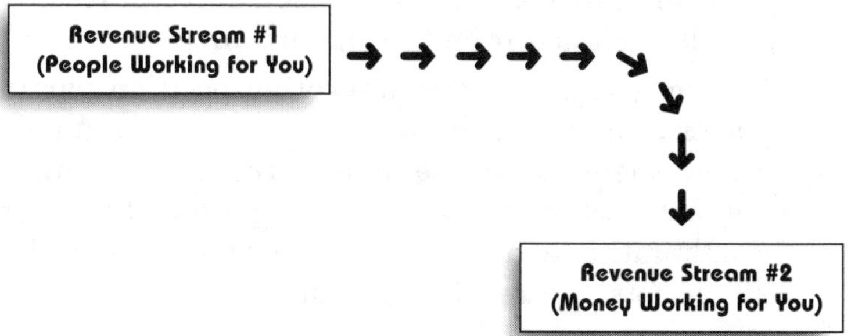

People can develop revenue stream #1 and use it as the feeding source for stream #2.

There are several ingenious aspects of network marketing worth noting as they relate to these two revenue streams:

- Network marketing is the epitome of stream #1. It allows participants to develop a team of like-minded entrepreneurs in an organization and profit from the team's collective success and productivity—"people working for them."
- Network marketing allows a person to develop a group of other people "working for them" without the endless hassles of hiring employees and running a traditional business. It is not the standard employer-employee relationship. It is a group of people playing on the same team and working together toward their common goals.
- Network marketing requires people to take an "equity position" in their business before stream #1 creates any significant revenue. But this is not based on financial equity; stream #1 is started and sustained with "sweat-equity." It requires participants to have an up-front investment of *time* and *effort* before significant revenue is produced on the backend. Anyone with a dream can capitalize their business and stream #1 with these two resources. No one is excluded from this opportunity.
- Not only can network marketing position participants to have people working for them, it can also allow them to have a *second* revenue stream of money working for them. It is a powerful and rare combination to have two sources of income-producing assets and residual income.

This unique opportunity to create two streams of revenue is often lost on people. Here is what I commonly see:

- Those who are not involved in network marketing miss the wisdom of creating a revenue stream of people working for them (stream #1). They also miss using this revenue as the feeding source of stream #2.

- Those who are involved in network marketing become so excited about the income it is creating that they overlook the power of using this revenue to start a second stream of residual income, i.e. having money work for them in stream #2. (This is a gentle way of saying they spend everything they make.)

Let me show you the power of having two streams of money work for you. If you are already in network marketing and you grasp what I am going to show you, you will discover that it is possible to be one of the highest income earners in your company via two income streams, even if you earn only a fraction of what "top income earners" make.

How Much Money Would You Like Working For You?

Determine the amount of money you would like to earn in the future with simple mathematics based on three variables: the money you desire to earn, the money you have saved/invested, and the rate of growth for your money. It looks like this:

If you want to earn	And your money is growing at an annual rate of	You need in savings/investments
$20,000/year	10%	$200,000
	20%	$100,000
$40,000/year	10%	$400,000
	20%	$200,000
$80,000/year	10%	$800,000
	20%	$400,000
$100,000/year	10%	$1,000,000
	20%	$500,000

If these sums look too staggering or too difficult to accumulate initially, remember "the rule of 72" to determine how quickly your money doubles itself. Let's assume that through your network marketing business you accumulated $50,000 in savings or investments and this money was doubling in size every four years. It would look like this:

$50,000 in Savings Doubling Every Four Years

Year 4	$50,000 becomes $100,000
Year 8	$100,000 becomes $200,000
Year 12	$200,000 becomes $400,000
Year 16	$400,000 becomes $800,000
Year 20	$800,000 becomes $1,600,000

Imagine someone being 25 years old and investing fifty thousand dollars that she earned in her network marketing business. If she did nothing else, she could have over one and half million dollars in savings/investments when she was 45 years old. If this money were earning ten percent per year, that individual would be receiving one hundred and sixty thousand dollars per year from this revenue stream. And this does not include the income she would also be receiving from her network marketing business every month. (If the money were earning 20 percent per year, the earnings would be three hundred and twenty thousand dollars per year without including revenue from her network marketing team.)

How old are you? What would happen if you set some financial goals of your own and began to relentlessly work your network marketing business to position you to earn significant revenue from stream #2 a number of years down the road? What if your goal was to simply earn twenty or thirty thousand dollars per year in residual income? When you begin to see how easy it is to have money work for you, it is far more motivating to work for the money that gets you started. Network marketing is your invitation to legitimate financial freedom, and the ability to *share* this concept is the next step.

Share the Strategic Value of Network Marketing With Prospects

Do you recall from chapter five that we need to "connect the dots" with prospects? That is, we need to remember how to relate our business to our prospects' lives, needs, hopes, and wishes. When we do this, our business becomes immediately relevant to them. How would you take the lessons in this chapter and make them pertinent to a prospect?

Following are some ideas you might want to consider as you focus on your audience, listen in 3-D, and speak as an ACE. You might ask or mention any of the following as a lead-in to create interest and start a fire:

- I know you work hard for your money. Have you ever found a way to have money work for you?
- After paying the bills, is it difficult to have any money left over to invest? Has anyone ever shown you how to begin to have money work for you even if you don't have any money to invest at this time?
- Have you ever thought seriously about when you want to retire and the income level at which you want to retire? Do you have a specific investment/retirement strategy that is working?
- I am forming an investment club with the goal of creating freedom of time and money for participants.

I am learning that it is far less difficult to create financial freedom than I ever knew. This investment club requires an up-front investment: not of money, but of time and effort.

- I used to dismiss network marketing as a silly attempt to create a small trickle of income. I thought it was an industry full of hype and lacking in substance and professionalism. Now, I am beginning to see that it is a realistic strategy for creating freedom of both time and money. Has anyone ever taken the time to show you how and why network marketing works?
- If I could show you a way to have both people and money working for you to relieve your financial pressure, would you be interested?
- I am just discovering that it is very feasible and easier than I knew to retire early and live well. I now have a realistic strategy and timetable to make it happen.
- Too many people spend their lives looking for a way to get rich quickly. I don't do that any longer. It is not realistic. I have found a way to get rich slowly. It is real, it works, and I now have a game plan and strategy to create my own financial freedom.
- If there were a way to work your butt off for a handful of years and then be financially free for the remainder of your life, would it be worth looking at?

It's Okay to Begin With a Utilitarian View

For intellectual, economic, social, and psychological reasons, I am a strong proponent of network marketing. I love the industry because I see it as a forum where all people are welcome to come and live as entrepreneurs and develop strategies for freedom of time and money. But you don't have to like network marketing to do it!

The next time you are in your car at the beginning or end of a workday, look around. How many of the commuters in the cars around you went to work that day because it is positively the most wonderful, fun, exciting thing that they can imagine doing? Not many. Most go to work because they have to do it. It is necessity that makes them show up. Work is a means to an end. Unfortunately, their work routine never stops because they never create an adequate source of income producing assets.

"Network marketing requires an up-front investment of time and effort."

It's okay to look at network marketing as a means to an end as well. It is a vehicle to get you where you want to go in life, to reduce stress, to end the grind of being an employee, and to give you freedom of time and money in the future. But you don't have to love the vehicle. All you need to do is love the strategy. Love network marketing as a means to an end. Love where it is taking you. Love the rare genius of having two streams of revenue work for you. Love the joy of hope. Love the joy of helping others.

Along the way, you will discover some of the finest people you will ever meet. You will develop some very close friendships, learn to be a team player, and learn to live as an entrepreneur. You will learn to work hard, be tough, and taste a quality of life you never thought possible. With these experiences, you might learn, accidentally, to love network marketing.

In the meantime, quit worrying about how much you enjoy the daily grind of growing your business. Accept the daily reality of what is required to be successful in life and pay your dues. Learn to:

- *Find joy in your dream.*
- *Find joy in your self-growth and discovery.*
- *Find joy in learning to manage fear.*
- *Find joy in learning to be a leader.*
- *Find joy in small successes and small earnings that are the precursors of more to come in the future.*
- *Find joy in having found an industry and a company that allow you to affiliate with them while giving you the freedom to dream, work, and succeed at your own pace.*
- *Find joy in an industry that will never put a ceiling on your success or earnings.*
- *Find joy in having a vehicle and a strategy for success that keep you progressing toward freedom of time and money instead of a life in which these things are hoped for but never attained.*
- *Find joy in being alive.*
- *Find joy in the journey to success.*
- *Find joy in being courageous enough to live life on your terms.*
- *Find joy in who you are, where you are going, and what it will bring you.*

Remember, you don't have to "like" network marketing to do it. But you do have to do it to get where you want to go and to get what you want in life. If you see the wisdom of golf course economics and having people and money working for you, then you will understand the simple genius of network marketing. Then the question you need to ask yourself becomes, "Now that I 'see it' what will I do about it?" May you be smart enough to "see it," seize it, and never stop.

CHAPTER
TEN

THE HIDDEN DIGNITY OF NETWORK MARKETING

Network marketing... it is a business that offers a second income, second career, second chance, second shot at success, and second shot in life. But there is one thing network marketing is not—it is *not* a second-rate industry. It is a first-rate industry and far more substantive than many people know.

While the economic potential of network marketing is well documented, the dignity of our industry often goes unnoticed. In my opinion, there are seven areas of hidden dignity that should be regularly discussed, consistently taught, and highly esteemed. They are reminders of why networkers should hold their heads high, speak with authority, and be proud of their participation in network marketing.

THE HIDDEN DIGNITY OF NETWORK MARKETING LIES IN...

1. The power of legitimate hope.
2. The unique criteria for admission.
3. The freedom to work part-time.
4. The power of preparing for retirement.
5. The power of stress reduction.
6. The power of respecting awesome talent and potential.
7. The sociological power.

1. The Power of Hope

Initially, I felt foolish. I knew I was playing a sucker's game. I was aware that the mathematical probability of winning was less than my chance of being struck by lightning. But when I thought about what I had to lose, there were only two things at risk: a few bucks and a couple of hours. Having both of these in adequate supply, I decided to play. So I got into my car, made the 30-minute drive, stood in line, and waited an hour for my turn to purchase a lottery ticket. Surprisingly, it turned out to be one of the most profitable hours of my life—not because I won the Powerball jackpot of 295.7 million dollars, but because I was reminded of the power of hope.

The line to the ticket window was a block long. People came from all over the Washington DC metropolitan area and surrounding states. Many had risen in the middle of the night to drive five and six hours to purchase their lottery tickets. Upon arrival, the pattern was the same for most people—we would silently take our place in the line, preparing to wait for the next hour, then notice that the people ahead in line were smiling, upbeat, and making eye contact with those around them; someone would invite the new arrivals into the conversation by asking how long they had driven, where they had come from, etc. Before long, most of the people in line were talking, sharing, and laughing like old friends—the fact that we were people from all over the world and all walks of life quickly blurred. A person's culture, color, or economic stature had no bearing on their acceptance into the conversation. All were welcome. When each of us finally got our turn to purchase a ticket, all the others offered a wish of good luck before saying goodbye.

As I drove home, I marveled at what I had just observed: the profound impact of hope in human beings. From the time these people waited in line until they discovered who won, they were infused with hope. For one brief moment, their dreams seemed possible—and the simple possibility of financial freedom, as remote as it was, brought out their best. It changed their disposition. It lightened the weight of their worries. And it released within them a freedom to be more of who they really were: kind people with good hearts and a desire to laugh at life and enjoy those around them.

Admittedly, the lottery offers a hope that is irrational, improbable, and short-lived. Since most participants know this, why do they play? They play because slim hope is far more bearable than no hope. Psychologically, there is a vast difference between these two views of life. Having spent a lifetime counseling on the most personal levels of human interaction and candor, I know the horrific damage that feeling stuck, trapped, and hopeless in life can wreak in a person's life. I have also witnessed the transforming power that comes from a person discovering hope.

In contradistinction to the lottery, network marketing gives people legitimate hope by offering a *mechanism* for seeing their hopes become reality. It is a business that allows individuals to actively participate in the attainment of their hopes and dreams, rather than leaving them to chance. To me, it's an honor to be involved in such an industry.

2. The Unique Criteria for Admission

It was her first job interview. While the adrenalin flowed, she tried to clear her mind, calm her nerves, and contain her excitement. I coached her on a few things that she might say, do, and ask. I drove her to the mall, walked with her to the clothing store, and waited outside as she entered. From there on, my 15-year-old daughter was on her own. She would have to meet the store manager, make her own introduction, and think for herself with no help from me. When she came out 30 minutes later, she gave me "the look" that said, "I got the job!" When we were no longer in view of the store, we laughed, hugged, and high-fived each other. Then we went out to dinner to celebrate and relive every exciting detail of her interview. When we got home, I don't know which of us was more excited and proud, her or me—I just know it was a great day for both of us.

Of course, not all job interviews have happy endings. For many people, looking for a job feels demeaning and produces only anxiety. The experience leaves them feeling powerless, vulnerable, and small. Their age, education, previous employment and salary, along with past accomplishments and future aspirations all become subject to the interviewers' critique. On the basis of a few minutes and a little information, the interviewers decide if the applicant is deemed "worthy" to come and work for them at a salary level predetermined and not likely to change significantly.

Against this backdrop, network marketing is wonderfully refreshing. It is a world in which the criteria for admission are positively unique. These criteria honor rather than dishonor people. They instill dignity rather than take it away. And they empower rather than disempower people.

Look at the difference between the expectations of a job interview and the criteria for involvement with network marketing.

In a job interview, they want to know:	**In network marketing, they want to know:**
- your academic degrees	- your degree of desire
- your education and experience	- your earnestness and excitement
- the income you have earned	- the income you want to earn
- your past accomplishments	- your future aspirations
- your curriculum vita	- your vision
- the résumé of your life	- if you want to resume life
- what you have done	- what you dream of doing

The traditional benchmark indicators of employability are of little value in network marketing. Neither admission nor success is based on age, education, previous employment, or impressive credentials. Instead, the litmus test of admission and potential in network marketing is more like getting a brief physical. All that is necessary to check are the eyes, heart, and hands. The eyes need to be checked for clear vision; the heart needs to be checked for its level of passion; and the hands need to be checked for calluses—to be sure the applicant is not afraid of hard work.

The next time someone you care about goes for an interview and is told that he or she is not qualified, stop and observe how it impacts that person's sense of security, esteem, and joy—then you will know another reason why I appreciate the hidden dignity of network marketing.

3. The Power of Part-Time

Mary was dressed up, wanting to look and be her best for the interview. She knew she was perfectly qualified for the job. As expected, the interview was going extremely well. Mary could sense that Leslie, the interviewer, liked her and wanted her to come and work with her firm. Finally, Leslie made her the job offer. With the offer on the table, Mary began to share some of her requirements before accepting the position.

First, she mentioned that she only wanted part-time employment. Leslie was caught off guard by the request, but she quickly recovered. She told Mary that she preferred a full-time employee, but would allow her to work part-time because she fit in so beautifully with her firm.

Emboldened, Mary proceeded to describe her conditions of employment in more detail. She wanted to work part-time, but the number of hours she would work each week would vary depending on other interests and responsibilities in her life. Some weeks she might work 20 hours, others she might work only three. Additionally, not only would the number of hours vary, but *when* she worked would as well. She explained that some days she may work only in the morning, others perhaps in the middle of the afternoon, and still others she might choose to work in the evening. With the convenience of modern technology, she added, she expected to work out of her home rather than Leslie's office. She saw no need to make a daily commute to the office, which was clearly an inefficient use of her time and energy.

Next, she told Leslie that she was only looking to earn several hundred dollars a month for some supplemental income. She was not looking for a career and did not want this job to consume her life. She had other interests and priorities. Knowing her own competence, though, she added that she *did* want unlimited income and leadership options just in case she decided to take this job more seriously in the future. Lastly, Mary mentioned that she wanted to take a vacation when she wanted to based on the rhythms of her family schedule.

"Network marketing offers people a mechanism for seeing hopes become reality."

Leslie attempted to conceal her bewilderment. She told Mary that she would think about her employment criteria and then notify her in a few days.

When Mary left, Leslie could not contain herself. She called in several of her colleagues in senior management and told them about the interview. They all had a great laugh hearing about this woman's preposterous expectations. Imagine someone wanting to be at home and work varying amounts of time each week at random hours of the day! Imagine having your work revolve around the other interests and priorities of your life! Imagine expecting to take a vacation when you want to! Imagine applying for a job and openly admitting that you only want to earn supplemental income and that this job will not be the dominant focus of your life! Imagine thinking you can work part-time but expect to have unlimited earning and leadership opportunities if you decide to become more serious about work in the future! The more this group talked about Mary's terms of employment, the harder they laughed. Eventually, the impromptu meeting broke up and the employees returned to their offices, secretly wishing what Mary was looking for was available in the real world.

On the way home from the interview, Mary picked up her cell phone and called Julie, a close friend. It was clear to Mary that the job offer had now been retracted. As she told Julie about the interview and her requests, they also started to laugh. They were laughing so hard that Mary had to pull her car off to the side of the road. They knew how preposterous Mary's candor appeared to Leslie, and that there was only one place where all of Mary's terms of employment would be respected and accepted as perfectly normal: network marketing.

4. Preparing for Retirement

John is still mystified by what happened. As he waited to make a left turn into the busy intersection, he knew the sun was obscuring his vision. He looked carefully, was confident that no cars were coming toward him, and made his left turn. Next thing he knew, he woke up in the hospital. He had been hit broadside by a truck he never saw approaching.

For many people, this is what preparing for retirement feels like. They've been "trying" to prepare for it, they know it is approaching, but it still seems a safe distance away; then, to their horror, they realize it is coming at them much faster than they expected. They cannot get out of its way and are hit broadside with three realities: time is moving more swiftly than they ever imagined; retirement is racing toward them; and they are not financially prepared for its sooner-than-expected arrival.

Network marketing offers a practical solution to people in this predicament. Those who consistently and effectively grow a successful business can, in a few short years, make up for the time they have lost. They can create a revenue stream of residual income that prepares them for retirement without dread of its arrival and without having to work more years than they preferred. I have great respect for the impact that an extra four hundred or four thousand dollars per month can have on one's quality of life in retirement. For some people, this makes the difference between having to work past retirement age or not, keeping their home or selling it; it can mean assurance of adequate medical care or the funds to enjoy themselves and avoid poverty.

Jim was in his mid-forties when he got involved in network marketing on a part-time basis. I knew he had a good career and a job that paid quite well, so I asked him what motivated him to jump into this industry. He laughed and said, "I like my job and it pays well, but I am working on the 40-40-40 plan. I will work 40 hours per week for 40 years. At the end of that time, I will retire and receive only 40 percent of what I have been earning. I want to retire without having to drastically change my lifestyle!" Jim is a wise man.

5. The Power of Stress Reduction

The dubious honor currently belongs to the United States: Americans now work longer hours than any group of people in the world. The statistical average is currently 1,965 hours worked per year. Consequently, stress plays an increasingly significant role in the lives of many people—whether we are looking at coronary disease, accelerated aging, diminished health, road rage, strained relationships, or overall life quality. You don't need me to give you the statistical data or the latest research to verify the impact of stress. Just look at your own life to observe how increased stress can change your response to everyday experiences.

Imagine that you get an unexpected $750 repair bill on your car and consider two different scenarios. In the first, you have $200 in your checking account and you are fearful of putting more debt on your credit card. In the second scenario, you have $7,000 sitting in your checking account and no credit card debt. How does each of these scenarios affect your response? In the first scenario, an unexpected $750 bill is a major problem that further exacerbates your sense of feeling stressed and trapped. In the other, it is simply an annoyance that you accept as part of life. You pay it and don't think twice about it.

Imagine that you have a four-year-old child who has just spilled a cup of milk for the third time at the dinner table. In one scenario, you have already had a difficult day. Before the meal, you are feeling fatigued, frustrated, and stressed about numerous things in your life. You are running on empty. In a second scenario, you are somewhat tired from the day, but not emotionally or physically spent. Does your own place in life determine how you respond to the milk being spilled for the third time?

Imagine driving to a very important appointment. You have been racing all day long. You are late in leaving for the appointment, traffic is moving slowly, and it seems that every traffic light is turning red just as you approach. Now imagine having had a day that was well paced, including plenty of time for driving to the appointment even if traffic is moving slowly. Do you respond differently in each case?

Most of us are well aware of the presence of stress in our lives. What is easy to overlook is how it *affects* us. Stress can cause sickness and reduce our ability to fight it, but long before it has done this, it has quietly been taking its toll in more insidious ways.

- Stress erodes our sense of humor and ability to see the lighter side of life.
- Stress diminishes our patience, our problem-solving skills, and our ability to effectively lead others.
- Stress lessens our ability to be playful.
- Stress lessens our ability to serve others.
- Stress lessens our ability to be gracious or understanding of others.
- Stress lessens our ability to be loving and forgiving.
- Stress lessens our ability to be ourselves and our best.

In short, when stress has been too acute for too long, it changes people. The finest parts of their personality, character, talent, and normal behavior can all be lost. While observers often notice this negative transformation, they are often at a loss in knowing how to help alleviate the stress. They simply try to cope with the change and hope that the behavior will somehow correct itself.

Why are unprecedented numbers of highly successful people leaving prestigious positions in the private sector to begin network marketing businesses? They want the quality of their lives back, they want their ability to laugh at life to return, they want control of their time, and they know that this is possible in network marketing. It is one of the unseen dignities of this industry.

6. The Power of Noticing Awesome Talent

When I travel and speak around the country, it is not uncommon for other practitioners in the mental health field to ask me why I no longer maintain a full-time private practice. My response is usually two-fold. First, I tell them that I have gone from private practice to "public practice"—I enjoy being able to impact large numbers of people through my speaking and writing. Next, I explain why I enjoy teaching entrepreneurs in network marketing.

In private practice, you hear and see people's most personal struggles. Any good clinician will care, commiserate, and coach people in ways to effectively manage their circumstances. But when someone is stressed because they just got downsized, have hit the glass ceiling, or have a boss that is abusive, when they are wonderful, gifted, and highly competent people but under-paid, under-valued, and under-appreciated, I want to do more than listen and give them coping skills. I want to offer them practical solutions. Thousands of people like this don't need therapy. What they need is a vehicle that puts them back into the game of life.

Where do you send individuals who never went to college or those who never graduated from high school? A quick glance at their modest résumés would give the impression that they lack intelligence, talent, or ambition. Consequently, in the job market they are promptly ignored. It is assumed that they have qualifications suitable only for some minimum-wage job. They cannot even get in the door for a preliminary interview, despite the fact that there are usually many legitimate reasons why they never graduated from high school or went to college—none of which reflect on their character, work ethic, or intellectual prowess. For example, as a child it is difficult to pay attention in school if you: go to school hungry; are sleep deprived because you work to help support the family; or if the chaos in your family is so disruptive that it inhibits your ability to concentrate.

"They need a vehicle that puts them back into the game of life."

Where do you send the "late-bloomer" in life who had a developmental lag? They have awesome talent, a desire to excel, and no one to give them a chance at a significant job because the only thing astonishing about their grades from college is how bad they were. These grades may reflect delayed maturation, but not intelligence or current levels of desire.

What about those who grow up in a family that never emphasized the importance of education or monitored academic performance? What about those who are so extraordinarily bright that the slow pace of learning in standard education hinders their ability to remain mentally stimulated so they "check out" of the learning process? What about those who have Attention Deficit Disorder and find that, despite their intelligence, remaining focused is extremely difficult? What about those who are uniquely smart but test poorly or feel performance anxiety when they take an exam? What about those whose true genius is never detected via the standard measurements of intelligence?

"Network marketing does not overlook very capable people, it welcomes them."

In each of the above cases, there are two tragedies. First, these people are regularly dismissed from any entrée into higher paying or professional careers. They are not even given the chance to smell success, let alone taste it. Secondly, and far more importantly, many of these people begin to look at themselves and erroneously conclude that they are *not* bright or capable. They begin to doubt and dismiss themselves. This in turn destroys their confidence, hope, and ambition. All of this dismissal is based on early life performance that is not even remotely indicative of their true talent, desire, and potential.

Where do we send those who have not been in the work force for years because they were raising children, assisting elderly parents, or doing something other than a traditional job? Should we interpret their absence as lack of ambition or ability? Do we conclude they are only worthy of an entry level or menial job? Shall we overlook the latent talent within them?

What about those who were downsized at the age of 40 or 50? What about those who are 60 years old and still full of energy, focus, and a desire to be productive? These are some of the most seasoned, dependable, and competent people to be found in the work force, yet they are often subjected to age discrimination. As an executive coach and business analyst, I am frequently involved with Internet companies. I stand in awe of this industry and welcome the monumental changes this technology is bringing to the world, but what about the people whose professions, careers, and livelihoods have been replaced by new technology? It's one thing to talk about the necessity of these people "retooling" for another career, but it's quite another for someone who has to work full-time, is financially strapped, and wants to maintain some semblance of personal balance to be "retooled." Under these circumstances, it is not a simple thing to go back to school and learn all new skills in order to remain competitive in the marketplace.

These people need an arena in which their talents can be utilized, their skills appreciated, their worth compensated, and their dreams fulfilled. Counseling cannot give this to people. Network marketing can and does. If you spend time with the kinds of people I've listed above, you'll quickly see what incredible potential contributions to the work force are often being disregarded. Network marketing does not overlook or dismiss these very capable people—it welcomes them—and that is my favorite aspect of this industry.

7. Sociological Power

Two steps forward, one step back. Sometimes social progress seems outrageously slow. But there is one group of people having more of an impact in this area than any program developed by a government agency or school system—the people in network marketing.

May I suggest that the next time you attend a meeting of several hundred people in your network marketing company, just study the group. Forget about the business and just observe what you see happening. Notice the friendship, fun, trust, and openness in the group. Look at the individuals and do your own demographic analysis. You will see people of different ages, communities, colors, countries, and cultures. You will see people from opposite sides of a city and opposite sides of the world meeting, talking, and befriending each other. You will see polar opposites come together regardless of education, economics, and employment. Hang around long enough and you will see these people work, play, travel, eat, and dream together. You will see them begin to genuinely trust and enjoy each other.

This happens so naturally in network marketing that it is easy to overlook the extraordinary nature of what is occurring. Most of these people could have lived two miles apart from each other and never met, but in this industry, they meet and begin to know, like, and respect each other. It is another one of the hidden dignities of this life-changing industry.

Believe In Your Business

There is an enormous amount of hidden dignity in network marketing. As you grow your business, do so with pride. Do so with confidence. Do so with authority. Do so with dignity.

CHAPTER
ELEVEN

LEADER TO LEADER

Sometimes in the process of *building* a team, we forget to stop and remind ourselves what it means to *lead* a team. Following are some reminders to assist you as a leader. If you don't have a large organization or leadership position in your company yet, feel free to eavesdrop—it's never too early to think and work like a leader.

As a leader, what are you supposed to help people in your organization manage? Above all, help them manage their own vision, skills, and motivation. They need you to help them stay focused, on task, and ever increasing in competence and confidence. To do this, there are several things your team needs you to model in your own actions.

You need to model positive expectancy, realistic hope, hard work, and secure leadership.

Model Positive Expectancy

Positive expectancy is a belief that problems are solvable, success is inevitable, and the effort required to build a successful network marketing business is worthwhile. It is one of the greatest qualities you can model to others. It fills the air around you with hope and optimism.

People on your team will occasionally grow weary of waiting for their dreams to become reality. Their business will grow more slowly than they expected. This experience is universally common to entrepreneurs, but since many participants in network marketing have never started or run a business, they are unaware of this. When their vision is blurred and their confidence low, they will draw strength from the clarity of your vision and the confidence you portray. Your belief will be the only thing that keeps them going at times. Make sure they see a belief in you that is strong, a vision that is clear, and a will that is resolute.

If your tendency is to view the world as a negative place where the sky is falling, the glass is half empty, and good things never last, be aware that this attitude kills optimism and momentum. Effective leaders don't poison the seedbed of hope that produces dreams, diligence, and success. They fertilize it with a vital component of effective leadership… positive expectancy.

Give Hope, Not Hype

Modeling positive expectancy is vastly different from giving people false expectations. It is fine to let others see your expectations for success, arouse their imagination and inspire vision, but don't get caught up in giving people *false* hope that is sure to be dashed.

In network marketing, if we "live by the sword, we will die by the sword." If we get people into the business by creating unrealistic expectations about the time, effort, or toughness required for success, we set them up for frustration, confusion, and disappointment. *The bigger the gap between what a participant expects and what they experience, the more likely they are to be disillusioned, discouraged, and then quit.* All because someone set them up with hype instead of real hope.

Be sure that you haven't unconsciously begun to promise more than our industry can deliver. When people wonder if they can make a specific amount of money within a certain time period—2, 6, 12, 24 months, etc.—it helps to give them a guideline for bringing balance to their expectations. You might show them the following continuum and help them to identify where their expectations fit into it depending upon the amount of revenue they hope to earn and the level of their efforts and skill:

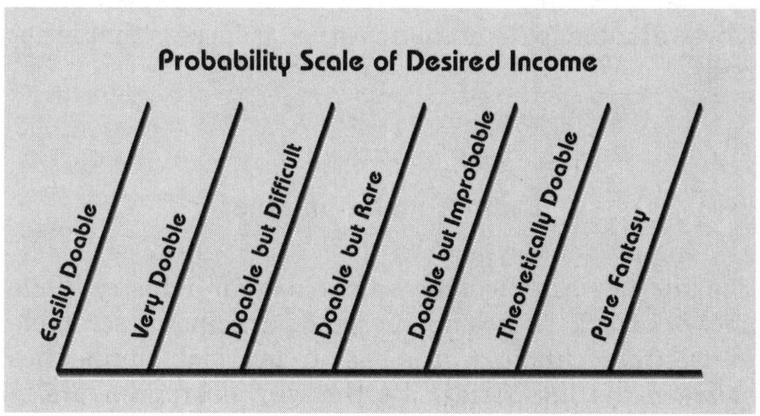

Not long ago, a network marketing company asked me to evaluate what was taking place in the field with its participants. During a round-table discussion, a top income earner spoke. He laughingly said, "I lie to people about how much money they can earn in a brief period of time and then I go home and repent." I cringed. The power and potential of our industry do not need to be hyped. They just need to be explained.

Along with avoiding hype, don't fall into the trap of pretending to be earning more than you are. Don't "fake it 'til you make it." This not only creates false hope in others, it makes you live an inauthentic life. I've frequently met people who started in network marketing to get out of debt and stop living hand to mouth, but as they began to make money, they wanted to *look successful.* They spent money on fancy new cars, new homes, and other items they thought were the indicators of success. In the end, these purchases didn't increase their pleasure, they only increased their financial pressure! It put them right back where they started: broke, in debt, and stressed. Remember, you didn't get into this business to get into debt at a higher level or to increase your economic pressure. Modeling and teaching wisdom to your downline will be far more valuable to them than posturing success that is not real.

Learn from the Internet

The Internet is incalculably valuable to our industry. While network marketing companies and participants scramble to use the technology, it is easy to overlook similarities between the industries. (By the way, entrepreneurs in the Internet community often refer to themselves as "netpreneurs." I like the term, but it should be used to describe entrepreneurs in network marketing! We missed using this wonderfully descriptive term.)

WHAT DO THE INDUSTRIES OF NETWORK MARKETING AND THE INTERNET HAVE IN COMMON?

- Both industries are changing the way traditional business is conducted.
- Both industries have the capacity for global impact.
- Both industries are rewriting the rules of life in the work place.
- Both industries attract bright, capable, and creative people.
- Both industries naturally attract entrepreneurs.
- Both industries are rewriting the way participants are compensated.
- Both industries offer the potential for financial rewards that exceed what is the norm in the traditional work world.
- Both industries attract people who are willing to work for far less than they are worth on the front-end in order to reap significant returns on the back-end.

Think again about the last point: *willing to work for far less than they are worth on the front-end in order to reap significant returns on the back-end.* A common term in the Internet world, especially among start-up companies, is "twenty-four/seven." It refers to the collective willingness of people to work twenty-four hours a day/ seven days a week to accomplish their goals. In the Internet community, participants are willing to work extremely long hours while being paid very little money in the beginning. Why do they do this? Because they are willing to risk investing time and effort on the front-end for the chance to reap financial rewards on the back-end in the form of stock.

> ***"Don't sell hype. Share hope."***

This is precisely what we do in network marketing. We choose to invest our time and efforts heavily on the front-end for revenue on the back-end. As a leader, you need to help people in your organization understand how the strategy works—and then help them *work* the strategy! Don't sell hype. Share hope. And then model a positive mindset with a strong work ethic.

Use Your Time Wisely

A common point of confusion for network marketing leaders is deciding which downline members should get the benefit of their time. They wonder, "Should I give unlimited or equal amounts of time to everyone who calls me asking for it? Am I supposed to be available at all hours of the day? How much time should I give people? How often should I give them my time?" These are significant questions. I will address them more fully in an upcoming book devoted exclusively to the subject of leadership in network marketing, but for the moment, remember: your time and energy are limited.

Do not indiscriminately give large amounts of time to every person who wants a piece of you. It will wear you out, particularly as your organization grows. Give the best moments of your time to those who have the greatest desire for success and are most hungry and teachable, to those you believe have leadership potential, and to those who are already leaders.

As a leader, you are to give people *business* support, not become their life-support system. You are growing a business, not a counseling practice. Be cautious with those who want you to help them with the business of life instead of the life of their business. These people can siphon off the best parts of your day, energy, and thinking that should go to others who are ready to learn, go, and grow. In short, the overly needy can become overly greedy for your time and counsel. They will suck you dry. It is your responsibility to learn to limit the time you spend with these people. Be gracious, but stop wasting excessive amounts of time on the phone or in person with them.

Learn to Give Your Power Away

I regularly see leaders of growing teams killing themselves trying to single-handedly tend to every detail of a large meeting, even when they have several capable people who would gladly help. As a leader, look for opportunities to give *others* responsibilities that will stretch their skills and belief in themselves while freeing you up to do the things only you can do.

To do this, you need to learn to give your power away. Avoid being a control freak, reluctant to let anyone else manage something because he or she may not do it as well as or in the same way that you would. The more you groom others for leadership, the more quickly your organization will grow and take on a life of its own.

Leadership is an honor and a privilege. But leadership is not the place to have your needs met. It is a place where you focus on the needs of those around you. One of the most destructive things you can see in any organization, including network marketing teams, is a "leader" who

"Give praise, attention, affirmation, and honor to others."

uses the spotlight of attention as a means for meeting his or her own needs. These are the people who *need* to be upfront, in charge, on stage, and recognized at each event or their feelings are hurt. They need to be "the big dog."

Learn to be so secure in yourself that instead of seeking ways to get *into* the spotlight, you look for ways to not only get out of it but also give it to others. Stay alert for opportunities to give praise, attention, affirmation, and honor to others on your team.

Not long ago, I heard the story of a woman who gave the spotlight of praise and recognition away to others until the day she died. Stories of her life were recounted with joy and tears at her funeral. One story I hadn't heard before struck me particularly. A nurse who cared for her wept openly when told of her death. When asked why she felt so deeply for this woman she had gently cared for as an Alzheimer's patient, the nurse told her story. Because of the loss of memory from the Alzheimer's disease, this woman had no recollection of things she said even moments earlier. Consequently, every time this nurse walked into the room, the patient would exclaim again, "Oh sweetheart, has anyone ever told you how beautiful you are?" Disease may have taken this patient's mind, but it never squelched a lifelong habit of giving others the spotlight of praise and honor. Some people called this special lady Evelyn, some called her Evy, and others called her Eve. I called her mom.

Model Secure Leadership

Earlier in the book, we looked at what it means to find your voice and be an ACE. Learning to speak with authority, conviction, and enthusiasm is extremely important as your leadership role increases. But keep in mind that secure leaders learn to do this while also speaking with respect for others. Their leadership is not shame-based or abusive. On the other hand, when insecure people are in positions of leadership, they often forget this. In fact, the insecure leader often confuses being an ACE with another three-letter word that begins with "a" and sounds very similar. Don't make this mistake. Be secure enough to get out of the spotlight of attention and give your power away.

Pace Yourself

Sometimes leaders in network marketing give so much to others that they forget the importance of pacing their own efforts. While helping others manage their vision, skill, and motivation, it is easy for leaders to forget to take care of themselves. They try too hard to do too much. You cannot do it all. You cannot help, please, serve, and lead everyone. There is little value in serving your team so eagerly that you neglect yourself and your family.

To pace yourself, learn to set aside times that become nonnegotiable for you and your family. Get in the habit of preserving moments of each day, days of each month, and special days or events during the year that are personal and family anchors. Let these times be untouchable for all but the most urgent of reasons. When someone asks you to speak, do a three-way call, or meet with "a

> ***"Learn to set aside times that become nonnegotiable for you and your family."***

hot new prospect who could be huge" during the times you have set aside, give yourself permission to explain that you are unavailable. Hold your ground, set a boundary, and find an alternative time. Is this easy? No. Is it necessary? Yes. Your computer, pager, and cell-phone all have "off" switches, so remember to use them! It will help keep you "on" for the long haul.

How do you determine when it's time to work very hard and when it's time to back off a little? In this chapter, I have mentioned concepts that seem to contradict one another (i.e. be *willing* to work twenty-four/seven and *avoid* working twenty-four/seven.) To know what you should do, it helps to remember what I often remind entrepreneurs in the Internet and corporate worlds to keep in mind: The difference between a *lifestyle,* a *season of life,* and a *stretch of road.*

Some people fall into a *lifestyle* of working all the time. These people are classic workaholics who are clueless about any type of balance or pacing in their work schedules. Work is the predominant focus and joy in their lives, and anything else is a distant second often viewed as an intrusion that must be reluctantly tolerated.

A *season of life* is an extended period with a beginning and an end during which a disproportionate amount of time is dedicated to one task or objective. For example, this is what people do in graduate school. They willfully agree to a life that is "out of balance" for a period of time—two to four years—understanding that they will benefit from this investment of time and effort for the rest of their lives.

The concept of a season of life is very important for entrepreneurs in network marketing. It does take a concentrated, highly focused season of life to launch a successful business. Just as a jet burns far more fuel during take-off than it does while cruising at 35,000 feet, your business will need extra "fuel" in the beginning. But keep in mind that this is only for a season—don't get stuck living this way permanently! When you reach cruising altitude, have some fun, back off, and enjoy your success.

A *stretch of road* is a brief period of time during which someone works at maximum capacity on one task with little hope of balance in other areas of life. It is like an 800-meter sprint—once you get started, you don't stop until you're done. There are times when you have to "sprint" for several days or weeks, but don't turn this pace into a *lifestyle*. It will exhaust you and exasperate those who are hoping for some time with you.

As you pursue success in your business, be sure to pace yourself with a willingness to work hard for a season, sprint when necessary for a stretch of road, but also take adequate time to keep yourself and your family refreshed.

Do for Yourself What You Do for Others

While helping those in your downline to protect their vision, skill, and motivation, be sure to do the same for yourself. Surround yourself with people who will inspire and motivate you as you do for others. Study those in your company you would like to emulate to discover why they are effective as leaders and successful in the business. Keep listening, looking, and learning. Do the things common to all exceptional leaders: regularly listen to tapes; read good books; meet with other positive entrepreneurs; and use executive coaches to help you be your best.

WHY IS IT SO IMPORTANT TO PROTECT YOUR OWN VISION?

- *The more clearly you see it, the more confidently you will seize it.*
- *The more clearly you see it, the more authoritatively you will say it.*
- *The more clearly you see it, the more enthusiastically you will build it.*

CHAPTER
TWELVE

KNIGHT YOURSELF

Many people grasp the power of network marketing. They know it works. They know it has changed countless lives and has given people hope, freedom, confidence, friends, and a quality of life once thought impossible. They have come to the point of believing in the industry, believing in their company, and believing in the compensation potential.

There is only one final decision they have to make before they get started or begin to experience new levels of success—they have to decide if they believe in *themselves*. They have to decide if they believe they can *personally* be successful. This is the last hurdle they have to clear before they are free to run with confidence towards their dreams and goals. If you feel you have yet to cross this final hurdle, here are four action points that will help you to do so.

1. File a New Flight Plan

In aviation, pilots file a new flight plan with each flight. Before the plane taxis down the runway, its route and destination are predetermined. I suggest that you give yourself permission to do the same thing with your network marketing business. File a *new* flight plan and be clear about your destination. Write down how far you intend to fly and the reasons you want to fly there.

Unknowingly, many network marketers live holding their new dreams and aspirations in one hand and an old flight plan in the other. When push comes to shove, the old flight plan, with its predetermined destination, puts their lives on autopilot and overrides the new goals they envisioned. Some people, upon inspection, discover that the old flight plan they are living by is not only out of date, it is inaccurate and restrictive. More importantly, they are surprised to learn that some other "well-meaning" individual filed this flight plan on their behalf. This well-meaning person might have been a teacher, school counselor, coach, parent, spouse, etc. Perhaps the old flight plan suggests:

You will never fly very far.

You will never fly very high.

You will never fly very fast.

You will never reach your destination.

You will never lead a squadron.

You will crash and burn.

You will never even leave the runway.

For some people, their flight plans are now so familiar that they no longer even question their validity. If you are truly going to be your best in network marketing, you need to examine your current flight plan and give yourself permission to revise it at will. Following are two examples of flight plans that could have kept the recipients on a very short flight:

RICK: Rick vividly recalls being a young boy and driving in the car one Saturday morning with his father who was a mail carrier. They drove past a gated area surrounded by high walls and huge oak trees. Curious, Rick asked his father, "What's in there, Dad?" His father responded, "Don't you worry about what is in there because you will never be invited inside those walls. It is a private country club for rich people who golf."

DIANE: Diane and her husband were enjoying the fruit of their labors. They had dared to dream, worked hard, and begun to win. Not long after moving into their beautiful new home in Dallas, Texas, Diane's parents came to visit. After touring the home and walking around the backyard swimming pool her mother finally spoke. She turned to her daughter and asked, "What makes you think you have the right to be the first person in our family to be rich?"

What happened here for Rick and Diane? In Rick's case, his father gave him a flight plan with a clear message: We are not wealthy and *you* never will be. We are blue-collar people and *you* always will be. We are "lower class" and *you* will never be invited into the "upper class" crowd.

In Diane's case, her mother reminded her of the flight plan that was filed *for* her. It said, "You are not to exceed our family level of mediocrity. You have no right to fly at different altitudes than the rest of us. Get back here with the rest of the family in the flight pattern where you belong. Shame on you."

Do you doubt the power of such flight plans? After the comment from her mother, Diane's business went into a huge tailspin. In the end, she and her husband lost their dream home. It was not until Diane heard me speak that she realized what had happened. Unconsciously, she had obediently gotten back in line and started to fly with the old flight plan her parents had filed for her. Fortunately, Diane is back flying with her own personal flight plan and getting ready to soar and fly to new destinations once more.

As for Rick, he gave himself permission to file his own flight plan. He did not let the predetermined flight plan he'd been given become the final reality of his life. He established a new one that said, "there is no limit to how far or high I can fly." Rick just returned from two days of lodging, dining, and golfing at Augusta National. It is one of the most exclusive private golf clubs in the world and he was the guest of honor. He is a long way from the flight plan that was predetermined for him.

Make sure you have a flight plan that grants you clearance to fly at new heights and to new destinations.

2. Knight Yourself

When Elton John was a guest on *The Tonight Show* with Jay Leno, I listened with fascination as he spoke of being knighted by the Queen of England. It was, without doubt, a powerful and momentous occasion for this accomplished musician to kneel, be knighted, and then granted the title, "Sir" Elton John.

I was intrigued by one particular aspect of his story. The title that was conferred on him came from an *external* source and had a profound impact on his *internal* life. But let's face it, most people will never be asked to bow before the Queen of England and have her confer on them a title of nobility and honor. So what should the average person do against these unlikely odds? Wait a lifetime, as so many people do, for someone else (a parent, spouse, employer, teacher, etc.) to confer upon them dignity, competence, or some other valued trait?

"Stop waiting for someone else to knight you. Knight yourself."

My advice is simple: Knight yourself. Stop waiting for someone else to confer on you the things you need for personal dignity and public success. Stop waiting for someone else to confer upon you the courage, heart, and intelligence you need for success in life and in our industry.

Earlier in the book I mentioned the movie *The Wizard of Oz*. Do you remember what the lion, the tin-man, and the scarecrow each desired the Wizard to confer on them? The lion wanted courage, the tin-man wanted a heart, and the scarecrow wanted intelligence. How did the movie end? The Wizard of Oz conferred the desired quality on each character, but what he really did was tell them that what they had been so diligently asking someone *else* to give them *already lay within them*.

The same is true for you. The seeds of greatness are already within you. So stop waiting for someone else to confer on you the qualities necessary for you to be a winner. (And stop listening to those people who conferred upon you the qualities of a loser!) Knight yourself.

If you cannot accept the permission to knight yourself, then I suggest you go to someone with far more authority than the Queen of England. Go to the living God and ask Him to knight you with dignity, love, and competence. His response will be clear: "You already have dignity. You are created in my image. You are already loved. You have been expected, wanted, and loved before the foundations of the world. I have already endowed you with competence. You already possess all that is necessary for success in life."

After you allow yourself to be knighted, then rise and live with dignity, authority, and competence, not just because you believe in our industry, but also because you believe in yourself.

3. Watch Out for the "I Love You" Virus

You may recall the computer virus that was hidden in an email message entitled, "I love you." This computer virus was a modern-day, high-tech Trojan horse that caused billions of dollars in damage around the world. This virus was able to spread quickly because the message title was so positive that recipients were eager to open the email for its contents. Unfortunately, the message that appeared so positive was actually very destructive.

When you get serious about changing your life and living as an entrepreneur, you will be surprised how many people will send you the equivalent of an "I love you" message that does nothing but eat away at your aspirations, joy, and confidence. As these people remain stuck in bureaucratic time with a life going nowhere, they will confidently remind you why you need to think twice about this new way of life you are pursuing in network marketing. They will happily tell you about every negative thing they have ever heard or experienced about this industry.

> ***"...don't give others the power or authority to determine your life choices."***

Psychologically, there are several reasons why people send you destructive "I love you" messages. Some of the senders are sincere but misinformed about network marketing. Others are risk-averse by nature and cannot imagine doing *anything* that appears risky, so they want to pass on to you their extremely cautious way of life. Still others are simply negative about anything in life that would inspire hope and change. They are experts at being joy-stealers. A few have motives that are more pernicious... they don't want you to succeed and attain a quality of life that is better than theirs. But most of the people who will send you messages of doubt are honestly unaware of the simplicity of success, the power of network marketing, and what it means to learn to think and live as an entrepreneur instead of an employee. The have no clue about the power of golf course economics, and the power of combining two streams of residual income via network marketing.

"Most people are blind when it comes to thinking, living, and succeeding as entrepreneurs."

When anyone, including friends and family, sends you a message with a hidden virus that begins to erode your zeal or confidence, don't even spend two seconds trying to figure out the reason why. Instead, learn to ignore the message like an email message you never read. Don't listen to them. Dismiss them as entrepreneurial or economic advisors in your life. Since they don't live with the consequences of your life choices, don't give them the power or authority to influence your life decisions.

Remember that most people are blind when it comes to thinking, living, and succeeding as entrepreneurs. They have been groomed to be employees and trained for modest financial expectations. They expect to work for money until they retire late in life and they have no knowledge of how to have money work for them. They literally cannot see what you are so excited about. They honestly cannot get it, grasp it, or comprehend it. Learn to be comfortable with this reality.

Every day I run into people who are not entrepreneurs. They are good, hardworking people who have absolutely no idea how easily their current and future lives could change if they would build a team of other like-minded entrepreneurs. I don't get frustrated with these people, nor do I let them steal my vision for one moment. Instead, I think of my dad.

My dad was completely blind the last decade of his life. The only sight he had left was one small area about an inch in diameter in the far right corner of his peripheral vision. Amazingly, dad never complained about being visually impaired.

Over the years, I often asked my dad what it was like to know he was progressively going blind. I recall eating dinner with him as he fed himself. In the morning, I would watch him feeling around for his numerous medications without asking for help. I watched this stoic man hang on to the last vestiges of his independence and dignity until the day he died. But there is one thing I never did. I never wanted to be blind like my dad. I never thought that because he was blind, I should be blind too. I loved him, let him live his life, and thankfully lived mine in the world of the seeing.

This is precisely what I still do today. When I am with someone who is blind to what it means to think, work, succeed, and live as an entrepreneur, I never doubt my vision. I don't think that I need to be like them. I say a prayer of thanks that I can see things they do not and happily go on my way. When it comes to being an entrepreneur, you and I live in the world of the blind and disbelieving—if you can accept this fact, you will be unaffected by the doubters you encounter who try to pass you a virus hidden in a message that says, "I love you."

4. Watch Your Language!

There is one threat far more dangerous than both the "I love you" virus and the flight plans others filed on your behalf. It can be the things you say to or about yourself in the privacy of your own mind. The worst saboteurs some people encounter are themselves. Learn to watch your language! Watch what you say to yourself.

When I was a kid, I loved watching *Andy of Mayberry*. You have probably seen the show too. Do you remember how many bullets Barney was allowed to carry and where they were kept? Barney was allowed to carry only one bullet and he had to keep it in his shirt pocket. Why? Because Barney had a propensity for shooting himself in the foot!

I find that many people have the same problem as Barney. Many people hobble through the day because they keep shooting themselves in the foot with a loaded gun equipped with a state-of-the-art silencer—their own private thoughts. Their negative thoughts are just as debilitating as real bullets. No one can see the moment you wound yourself with a silent, dream-stealing, confidence-crushing thought. They only notice that you are not running at full stride and with full confidence in the game of life.

How Do You Stop Shooting Yourself in the Foot?

Have you ever purchased a new item of clothing, like a pair of slacks, and found in the pocket a little piece of paper that reads, "inspected by #146"? What is the job of inspector #146? It is to pay attention to each item of clothing that passes along the assembly line and examine it for defects. If a defect is found, the inspector deems the item unacceptable for sale and prevents it from going any further.

You need to be like inspector #146 with your thoughts. Learn to examine the thoughts that come down the assembly line of your mind. Inspect them before they have a profound influence on your inner emotions and outward behavior. If your thoughts are flawed, unhealthy, or toxic, then stop them from taking up space and remove them—deem them unacceptable. Remember, either you will learn to capture your thoughts or your thoughts will capture you. (For a review of this concept see chapter seven in *Dare to Dream and Work to Win.*) The most deadly things some people hear originate in their own minds.

Spend a Night at the Movies

Would you like to know what it is like to have a dream and succeed while living in a community, culture, and home where almost everything seems bent on preventing you from pursuing your dream? Rent the video, *October Sky.* This movie, although largely ignored by the critics, is a true story of a young boy growing up in the coalmines of West Virginia. It is the perfect portrayal of someone who dares to file a new and different flight plan and then finds himself ostracized, ridiculed, doubted, and resented for his seemingly preposterous goals. At almost every turn, people send him the "I love you" virus, telling him to accept the flight plan others predetermined for him. It is a powerful, poignant, and tender portrayal of what it is literally to want to reach for the skies when those around you want you to spend your life groveling in the dirt. Don't just casually watch this movie—study it. Then go write your new flight plan, stop reading emails with viruses, watch your language, and knight yourself.

CONCLUSION

DO YOU KNOW WHAT TIME IT IS?

I thoroughly enjoy helping people be their best. Whenever I'm working with others as an executive coach, I always remind them that I am nothing more than a coach on the sidelines. Like a coach for aspiring Olympic skaters, I will be at the side of the skating rink. I will study, observe, analyze, critique, encourage, and believe in them, but they are the athletes. They are the individuals attempting to learn new things, develop new skills, and reach new heights of accomplishment.

When the work is finished, it will be *their* honor. It will be *their* victory, *their* pride, and *their* satisfaction. They alone will stand in the winners' circle. They will stand on the platform and receive the gold medal as their national anthem is played and their flag raised. It is their dream, their work, and their victory. I am honored to simply stand in the wings and assist them. The work and the win, the guts and the glory, the pain and the prize

are theirs. Coaches have no place on the winners' stand in the end.

The time has come now for this coach to be silent and for *you* to get started. It is time for you to implement all that we have talked about in this book. To borrow a line from a country western song, it's time for "a little less talk and a lot more action."

It is time for you to begin working, thinking, and living as an entrepreneur instead of as an employee. It is time for you to stop thinking about the potential of our industry and start enjoying the benefits of it. It is time for you to stop wishing for success and to begin to enjoy it.

It is time to let your dreams fuel you, your focus guide you, and your belief in yourself and our industry empower you. It is time to embrace the simplicity of success.

It is time for you to knight yourself and file a new flight plan. It is time for you to ignore fear and block out the crowd. It is time for you to clear your mind, focus your thoughts, and suck up your gut. It is time to let yourself go, without reservation, in the direction of your dreams.

After much effort, you *will* climb the winners' platform. And when you do, I will find silent pleasure in having played a small part in your extraordinary success.

I just heard your name called . . . it's time for you to take center stage. It is your turn to perform. Break a leg!

The Barrett Bulletin

Free Entrepreneurial Insights and Encouragement

Let Tom Barrett help you and those on your team stay focused and motivated. Once a month via e-mail, Dr. Barrett sends out the *Barrett Bulletin* to entrepreneurs just like you.

To receive these free bulletins go to:
www.daretodream.net
and click "free newsletter"

You will start receiving encouragement to stay focused in your pursuit of success.

Ordering Information:

Order Online at www.daretodream.net
E-mail requests to: orders@daretodream.net

Title	Price
Dare to Dream and Work to Win Understanding the Dollars & Sense of Success in Network Marketing (Book)	$14.95
Dare to Dream and Work to Win Audio Book (4 CD set)	$24.95
Success Happens! Let It Happen For You In Network Marketing (Book)	$14.95
Success Happens! Let It Happen For You In Network Marketing Audio Book (4 CD set)	$24.95
Demystifying Success CD Series Cracking the Code on Life-Changing Confidence, Commitment, and Success in Your Business	$109.95
Win as a Team While You Dare to Dream! How to Win at Home and a Home-Based Business	Free download online

To order or for information about volume discounts, visit:
www.daretodream.net

Phone: **703-777-1007**

For information about having Dr. Barrett speak LIVE at your event:
703 777-1007
tom@daretodream.net

Ordering Information:

Order Online at www.daretodream.net
E-mail requests to: orders@daretodream.net

Title	Price
Dare to Dream and Work to Win Understanding the Dollars & Sense of Success in Network Marketing (Book)	$14.95
Dare to Dream and Work to Win Audio Book (4 CD set)	$24.95
Success Happens! Let It Happen For You In Network Marketing (Book)	$14.95
Success Happens! Let It Happen For You In Network Marketing Audio Book (4 CD set)	$24.95
Demystifying Success CD Series Cracking the Code on Life-Changing Confidence, Commitment, and Success in Your Business	$109.95
Win as a Team While You Dare to Dream! How to Win at Home and a Home-Based Business	Free download online

To order or for information about volume discounts, visit:
www.daretodream.net

Phone: **703-777-1007**

For information about having
Dr. Barrett speak LIVE at your event:
703 777-1007
tom@daretodream.net

From Author Dr. Tom Barrett

Dare to Dream and Work to Win

Understanding the Dollars & Sense of Success in Network Marketing

Discover: • How wealth is actually created • The psychology of personal success • How to think and live as an entrepreneur • How to effectively lead a downline • How to set realistic financial expectations • How to take charge of your life and future • How to succeed in direct sales. *Available in Book and Audio Book form.*

Success Happens!

Let it Happen For You In Network Marketing

If success is your destination then this book, the sequel to *Dare to Dream and Work to Win,* is the road map for you and those on your team. In this book discover: • Strategies for success in network marketing • How to get hot responses from your warm market • "15 minutes to financial freedom" • How to conquer fear and self-doubt • The unstoppable power of personal dreams mixed with personal focus • Golf course economics... The secret of building wealth. *Available in Book and Audio Book form.*

Demystifying Success

Cracking the Code on Life-Changing Confidence,
Committment and Success in Your Business

In this LIVE presentation on seven CDs, Dr. Barrett takes the mystery out of success. He examines and explains each critical component of your business. This comprehensive series is guaranteed to be extraordinarily insightful, entertaining, and motivating. It will also stretch your vision, increase your skills, and touch your heart.

Win as a Team While You Dare to Dream!

How to Win at Home and a Home-Based Business

Life is much more enjoyable when couples learn to work as a team while one or both of them is daring to dream. In this book, Dr. Barrett brings together years of experience as both a coach to entrepreneurs and as a "shrink" to help you achieve "balanced success."

Order Online at www.daretodream.net